VICTIM 2 VICTOR

The Inspirational True Story of a Courageous Woman's Struggle, with Sexual Abuse and Devastation, Until She Discovers the Path...
to Inner Peace

Anu Verma

Anu Verma

Victim 2 Victor
Copyright © 2020 by Anu Verma
All Rights Reserved

All rights reserved. No part of this publication may be reproduced, distributed, or transmitted in any form or by any means, including photocopying, recording, or other electronic or mechanical methods, without the prior written permission of the AUTHOR, except in the case of brief quotations embodied in critical reviews and certain other noncommercial uses permitted by copyright law. This book is not intended as a substitute for the medical advice of physicians. The reader should regularly consult a physician in matters relating to his/her health and particularly with respect to any symptoms that may require diagnosis or medical attention. Although the author and publisher have made every effort to ensure that the information in this book was correct at press time, the author and publisher do not assume and hereby disclaim any liability to any party for any loss, damage, or disruption caused by errors or omissions, whether such errors or omissions result from negligence, accident, or any other cause. Also, this story is based on real events; names have been changed to maintain anonymity, and the accounts have been written from the author's memory.

Publisher: Absolute Author Publishing House
Editor: Dr. Melissa Caudle
Associate Editor: Kathy Rabb Kittok
Cover Designer: Rebeca @Rebecacovers

Paperback ISBN: 978-1-64953-095-0
eBook ISBN: 978-1-64953-096-7

IN-PUBLICATION-DATA

Victim 2 Victor/Anu Verma

   p. cm.

   1. Self-Help   2. Overcoming Abuse   3. Self-Worth

VICTIM 2 VICTOR

Acknowledgments

My family, friends, and others whom I met along my journey have all helped me to get through the most challenging times. My life journey has led me to heal, to become the woman I was intended to become, and so much more. I thank you from the bottom of my heart for this. I couldn't have done it without you. Writing this book has also meant so much to me. It isn't possible to name everyone in this Acknowledgment, but if you are reading it, you will know how much you have helped me. You will be forever in my thoughts and prayers. Namaste!

A special mention to:

Rehannah Mian, who inspired me to strive to achieve my goals and to follow my dreams. It is because of Rehannah and her fantastic travel stories that I discovered my love of traveling. I will never forget her "elephant pants story," as she climbed the rocks in Australia. I can still laugh about this now. Even though I wasn't there when it happened, Rehannah made me feel as if I was.

Monica Dougall, for being my best friend. The one I could always turn to for help with any problem that I had, and who was there to celebrate my every success. During the darkest times, especially when I was going through so much turmoil in relationships, she encouraged me to keep going.

My dearest cousin, Anita Verma, for recommending Marie Scott, who also played an essential part in helping me to heal.

My cousin who was also the victim of abuse when we were little girls, and for whom I have enormous respect for. She grew up to lead a settled life with her partner and children.

I would like to thank my Mum and my Dad for giving me the strength to share my story with others. Also, my brother. Even though we haven't always been close, now that we are older and have become parents, our family bond has become stronger.

Anu Verma

Thank you to my dear friends Jasmine Heir & Lisa Bose whom I call my 'soul sisters,' I thank you both for introducing me to the teachings of Tony Robbins. The man who had a significant impact on improving the quality of my life and helping me to believe in myself.

Alex Roseman for coaching me and encouraging me to write my story even when I doubted myself, he would inspire me to keep writing.

I would also like to thank all the spiritual and supportive friends I have met along the way. Those who have inspired and helped me to believe in myself. Especially, Paramjit Pam Anand; David Challenor; Katrina Garg; Florina Borsan; Christina Nikoletti; Amina Yusufzai; Helen Jones; Maura Kwik; Melissa Ching; Goodie Pabla and Lyndsey Austin.

The teachings of the Dalai Lama and Buddhism have also helped me greatly. I know too that I wouldn't have been able to do this without Tony Robbins. The life lessons he taught me when I attended his seminars, personal development, and coaching courses. His books, audios, and podcasts that I often spent most of the day listening to.

I hope that this book, and my story, will help and inspire you to heal if that is what you need to do.

Without you, none of this would have been possible.

Much love to you all, Anu x

VICTIM 2 VICTOR

Table of Contents

Anu Verma: Victim 2 Victor   ix
Introduction ix
Healing   x
Part I: My Childhood Trauma   12
Chapter I: Abuse, Fear, and Guilt 13
Chapter II: Why Was This Still Happening to Me?   19
Chapter III: Wild and Crazy   24
Chapter IV: My Dark Life 27
Chapter V: Traveling   34
New Zealand   38
Cambodia   40
Thailand   41
Laos   44
Chapter VI: Returning to the UK 46
Chapter VII: My Life Is Like a Never-Ending Circle   50
Chapter VIII: A New Relationship and a Broken Dream   74
Chapter IX: Marriage   79
Noah   82
And Me Today   84
Sharing My Story   85
Chapter X: Therapy and a New Beginning   87
Gifts from Marie, My Therapist   87
The Tools Marie Gave to Me   89
I Also Discovered Tony Robbins   90
Part II: Abuse and Trauma   92
Chapter I: Abuse   93
Physical Abuse   93
Child and Adult Sexual Abuse   95
Psychological Abuse   96
Neglectful Abuse   97
Domestic Violence and Abuse   98
Chapter II: What is Sexual Abuse? 99

Childhood Sexual Abuse	101
Adult Sexual Abuse	104
Rape	105

Chapter III: What is Trauma? 107

What is Trauma?	107
Naming Your Trauma	109
Acute Stress Disorder	109
Post-Traumatic Stress Disorder (PTSD)	109
More Symptoms of PTSD	112
Psychological Trauma	112
Developmental Trauma	114
Vicarious Trauma	116
Historical or Intergenerational Trauma	116
Complex Trauma	117

Chapter IV: Easing the Pain of Trauma 118

Don't Feel Isolated	118
Understand What Happened	119
Seek Professional Help	120

Chapter V: Healing Trauma 124

Types of Therapies	126
EMDR or Eye Movement Desensitization and Reprocessing	126
Imagery	128
Writing	129
Psychedelic Therapy	130
System Desensitization	130
Behavior Therapy	131
Aversion therapy	131
Cognitive-Behavioral	
Cognitive Behavioral Play Therapy	132
Hypnotherapy	133
Exposure Therapy	139
Neurofeedback	139
Group Therapy	140
Acupuncture for Treating Trauma	141
The Essential Breath	141

Chapter VI: Treatment for Child and Adult Abuse 142

Treatment for Child Abuse	143
Therapy for Adult Abuse	147

Part III: Healing and Victory   149
How Traveling Helped me to Heal   150
What I Learned from Relationships   151
Life Skills which I Learned to Improve Relationships   154
Introduction to Energy Healing   **157**
Energy Healing Modalities   158
Chapter I: Reiki   159
   Chapter II: Yoga and Healing Powers   159
Yoga and Healing from Trauma   165
Yoga Poses for Healing Traumatic Experiences   168
   Chapter III: Emotional Freedom Techniques (EFT)   170
   Chapter IV: How Healing Shifted the Weight   177
Part IV: Making Decisions   185
Chapter I: Steps in the Decision-Making Process 186
Chapter II: The Dickens Process and Decision Making   189
Visualization Techniques: 199
Final Thoughts 204
My Life   205
Sexual Abuse and Trauma   206
ABOUT THE AUTHOR 210

Anu Verma

Anu Verma: Victim 2 Victor

No matter what I have been through, I am still here. This is my story of how I healed.

Introduction

There is light in the darkness. Even if it is only a flickering light, it is always there and grows. The more we tend to it. I know this because no matter what I have been through, I am still here, and I can share my story with you. If you are going through abuse or trauma as I did, this light exists, and it will remain with you until your journey leads you to a place of healing, just as mine did.

I am an Asian woman of Indian ancestry. I was born with black hair and lots of it. I was very fair-skinned for an Indian girl and developed to be a tall woman with a height of five feet eight inches. I took after my mother, who was very pale and so she didn't have any trouble finding a husband at sixteen as there was a queue of potential partners willing to take her hand in marriage. Myself at sixteen, I didn't feel so worthy, and I had put on weight because of overeating and secret-eating. It was my way of comfort to cover the pain that I felt inside as I had suffered sexual, physical, and mental abuse as a child and which continued into my teenage years, and as a young adult.

I longed to talk to my mother about my feelings of hurt and betrayal that I was suffering. I wanted to open my heart and soul to her and be comforted by her in return. However, the need to talk through problems was suppressed in our Asian culture. We didn't discuss feelings. Everything we did was based on status and reputation, which didn't include publicizing our private affairs. As this was firmly adhered to in my culture, I experienced difficulty in letting my family know what I had gone through at a young age, especially since one of my sexual abusers was also a relative. When I finally told my parents what he had been doing to me, I was instructed to act as if nothing had happened. I know now that this was wrong to push these incidents "under the carpet." Being unable to acknowledge and to talk about the abuse were two of the principal reasons I struggled for so many years to heal myself.

When I was growing up, this situation led me into many relationships with men who were as needy as I, and who abused me. They scorned whatever I did, which increased my feeling of worthlessness, and I lost all sense of belonging. I became confused. I drifted even further toward them, hoping that this would help me. I describe the struggles which I experienced with these men in this book. In reality, it took years of therapy, self-help motivation, and tending the light within to rid me of these negative feelings.

I am writing this book now, with a sense of joy and freedom, that I have been able to overcome the intense feelings which this trauma caused. Until I was strong enough to seek the therapy I needed from a dedicated professional, I was overwhelmed by fear, distrust, rejection, low self-esteem, being powerless, and isolated. These thoughts and emotions ran through my mind almost continuously, from when I was three. The self-awareness programs of Tony Robbins and training to become a Reiki Master and a yoga teacher also helped me to find my true self-worth.

So, I have changed. I am now a strong, determined, and resilient woman. I am no longer a victim but a victor who has accomplished a great deal. Through hard work and determination, I gained a Master of Science degree and traveled worldwide twice. I have also developed a successful career in sales and education as well as becoming an author. My most notable achievement to date is that I am now a mother. My beautiful son, Noah, was born in 2018.

Healing

Energy healing is an alternative medicine based on the belief that vital energy flows through the human body. It is a holistic practice that helps us activate our body's healing power by removing energy blocks. My therapist helped me spiritually and taught me to use healing energy and tapping techniques. She gave me the tools to change my thoughts, realign my emotions, and realize that I didn't need to rely on others to be complete. I switched from trusting the wrong people to appreciate and value myself and my true self-worth. She also showed me I deserved to be happy and loved. I became a Reiki Master, embracing its philosophies, and I learned the healing discipline of yoga.

I attended seminars and classes given by Tony Robbins, also known as Anthony J. Mahavoric, an American author, philanthropist, and life coach. Tony's ambition and drive helped me gain further insights into what had influenced my decisions. When I attended the seminars, I reset my beliefs about my self-worth and esteem. I could release the negative thoughts which ran through my mind. His seminars, books, and lectures gave me the tools to make the right decisions for me.

I will tell you more about the origins of my trauma in this book. How I responded to the challenges this presented, and how my therapist helped me heal. I will also talk about Tony Robbins and how his energy and knowledge changed my life.

I hope you will read my book with an open mind and be prepared to understand my journey. It may inspire you and show you how to heal so you, too, can overcome the challenges life has thrown at you. You can become a victor as I did.

Anu Verma

Part I: My Childhood Trauma

VICTIM 2 VICTOR

Chapter I: Abuse, Fear, and Guilt

I came into this world on June 25th, 1980, in Coventry and was brought up in the United Kingdom. My parents were born in the Punjab area of India. They moved to the UK when they were teenagers intending to make a better life for their family and themselves. They lived at a close relative's house with him and his wife and their two children. They were sleeping on a mattress on the floor in the spare room with nothing to their name. When they finally saved up enough money to move out, it was into a two-bedroom terraced house in the inner city of Coventry. My mother was eighteen years old when I was born. I also have an older brother, eighteen months older than me. Looking back, I can see how tough life must have been for our mother with two small children at such a young age. She didn't have the skills to deal with the society in which she found herself and its influences. As a child, she had been subjected to Indian culture, where women have specific roles. They are expected to look and behave in particular ways, while men are in control of the family and society. It was different in the United Kingdom.

Margaret Thatcher was Prime Minister in the 1980s. The laws and socially acceptable behavior for women had changed, giving them a more prominent role in the home and workplace. Immigration was also under review. She promised to drastically reduce the number of Commonwealth immigrants who, like the members of my family, were arriving in the United Kingdom. She held the belief that foreign influence was harmful to the British way of life, and so many immigrants suffered from racial abuse and discrimination. Even though we lived in a multicultural area, my family was often referred to as Asian, or Indian, rarely British. It was common for families of the same ethnic culture to build communities where they lived, as it gave a sense of security and familiarity.

Many had embraced Margaret Thatcher's policies, which led to poor working conditions for immigrants, and with the locals looking down on us. On shopping trips in the city center, back in the 1970s, my mother and father were called 'Pakis' and were told to go back to their own country and not welcome in the UK. This abuse was mainly from the neo-Nazis, who were also termed the skinheads. My parents had come from Punjab, North India though, we are all still seen as Pakistanis. The abuse only bought my parents closer together, and they have maintained a powerful bond throughout their life. I can't help but think it was the struggles they had overcome together, which grew their resilience and strength and a solid foundation to raise their family.

I also experienced what I call indirect discrimination, even though it was never directly to my face. An incident which I will never forget, occurred while in primary school. I had received some sterling silver jewelry for my birthday and wore the beautiful necklace, earrings, and bracelet to school the next day. I was told by the headteacher to remove my jewelry because we could not wear any, so I placed the jewelry into my bag on a peg outside of my class. When it was home-time, I saw that my beautiful pendant, earrings, and bracelet were gone. It devastated me. I had an idea of who had stolen it – a boy named Greg in my class was known for stealing from everybody. After the initial shock, I cried because I was so hurt that I hadn't even worn my jewelry for more than a day. I went to my teacher, who took me to the head-teacher, and I explained what had happened and that I knew who had stolen my birthday gift. The children had already left for the day, and the teachers wanted to go home, so there was nothing they could do. Now I felt like a burden, a pest, and a reason her dinner would be late.
My feelings of loss didn't seem to matter to anyone, maybe because I wasn't English. Perhaps because I wasn't worthy of their time?

VICTIM 2 VICTOR

Whatever it was, that feeling of worthlessness stayed with me for many years. Greg had gotten away with it. I still feel that more could have been done about this in terms of an investigation, though there was nothing. I felt defeated, and like I didn't matter.

I have some good childhood memories, such as my doll, whom I called Kay. I loved her dearly, and the days when we played outside. Kay was a gift to me from my parents when I was born. She still had my hospital birth bracelet on her wrist. She was a beautiful white doll and was maybe brought into my life to signify the beauty of being white. I would play with Kay in my bedroom, and she had her little cot, and I treated her like a baby. I would feed her milk from her bottle, hug her, and care for her; it was such a beautiful connection that I felt with Kay and one that I would cherish forever. These memorable childhood moments sadly didn't last.

As a child, you have the right to be cared for, protected, and loved. When I was only three or four years of age, I no longer felt safe, and my innocence had been taken away from me. Gary, a tenant who rented a room at our house, sexually abused me. Gary used to open my bedroom door during the night. He would creep inside, hold my head, and force me to touch and lick his genitals. I learned from him as a tiny child how to perform oral sex and how to masturbate someone.

Gary also used to creep into my bedroom when my family's friends were there. This did not stop him from entering my room. Gary coerced me into performing indecent acts on him, so I felt guilty and confused afterward. I understood that what I had been made to do was wrong, and I was frightened. He was an adult, so I had to obey. He told me it was our little secret, so I shouldn't tell anyone, or there would be terrible consequences for my family and me.

My parents should have been able to trust him as an adult and a friend of the family. This experience also taught me how to be deceitful. I would pretend to be asleep, hoping that he would decide not to awaken me. I didn't scream or cry out for help. I did as I was told, and I didn't tell anyone about it at the time. In reality, no child should have to remember the sight and smell of a naked man who forced her to pleasure him.

To this day, I can still vividly recall what happened, despite the many years of therapy. I can continually associate the pervading smell of his genitals with those of my partners. It isn't difficult to understand why my later relationships failed. Gary's abuse was always at the back of my mind, and I have struggled with intimacy for most of my life and sex became a form of play-acting for me. I even compared it to a game of Twister, although I regarded it as dirty. However hard I tried, I couldn't associate sexual intercourse with love.

I let it happen, without knowing that I had a choice. It made me feel empty on the inside as if I had exposed my inner self to the world, and it was very raw. I realize now that I played right into his shame. The more ashamed I felt, the more power he had over me. I was living in a dark place. I no longer smiled and laughed. Yet, no one seemed to know or understand what was wrong with me or even care. After two years of this, I told another close female relative who I felt I could confide in. You have to understand how hard this was for me in my culture, being in the 80s, shame-fueled, fearful of the consequences, yet I found the strength. I cried when I told her what was happening. I described the things Gary made me do. I said that he would do bad things to my family and me because I had spoken to her, but it had reached the point where I had to tell someone. My heart was breaking.

My female confidant was appalled, shocked, and furious. She had no idea what Gary had been doing, nor did the rest of our family. She cried with me that day and assured me she would speak to my parents. They threw Gary out of our house after what must have been two or three years of abuse, and what a happy day that was for me! I can't remember getting any extra attention from my mum afterward, but I was so relieved that he had gone. The sun had come out again, and I could enjoy being a young girl again.

I Was Still Only A Child...

VICTIM 2 VICTOR

Being sexually abused at three years of age was traumatic, and it got worse when it happened again at seven. This time my abuser was a trusted relative from India. He often visited my family, and although I can't recall the exact time it lasted, I believe that the abuse went on for about a year. I can still vividly remember an incident when he quietly opened my bedroom door, and I had fallen asleep. He got into bed with me, put his hands inside my pajamas, and caressed me.

As a child, I used to have to pretend to be pleased to see him. His visits felt like a form of torture. I believed that when he looked at me, I felt like he intended to molest me later. I tried not to stay in the same room as him. I didn't feel able to run away from home, as I knew how much this would alarm my family. That was the light still burning within me, but I couldn't help my emotions switching off after a while. I could not even bring myself to be affectionate to my parents, and especially my brother, who had by now become distant.

I learned to hide how I was feeling. When I was in my room at night, I pretended to be asleep. I froze as I did when I was younger, hoping again that my abuser would go away. I tried to show him I enjoyed his visit when I was with my family, but deep inside, I was crying. It was so sad that at such a young age, I had to learn to lie to protect myself and my family.

"Look who has come to see us, Anu. Isn't that nice?"

"Yes, Daddy," although what I really meant to say was, "not really, Daddy."

"Why don't you show him your picture from school?"

"Yes, Daddy," even though what I meant was, "no thanks, Daddy. I don't want to spend a second longer than I have to in this room."

"Why are you shy?" my Dad asked.

"Sorry, Daddy," though what I really wanted to say was, "because I don't want him to think that I like his attention, Daddy."

This situation brought more confusion and pain. A child isn't prepared for repeated sexual stimulation. Even if I didn't know precisely why it was wrong, I developed emotional problems that have haunted me my entire life. I suffered low self-esteem, feelings of worthlessness, and a distorted view of sex. I became withdrawn and mistrustful of adults.

I pushed myself instead to get good grades and to do well. I was desperate to do something which would make my family proud of me and to love me. However, all this had caused me to make poor judgments throughout my life. I always felt ashamed, guilty, afraid, and angry. I had no idea when I was seven years of age that what I was suffering from had a name or was even something for which I could get help. All I knew was that Gary and my relative had hurt me badly, physically, mentally, emotionally, and that there was no one there to soothe the pain.

Children who are abused and traumatized keep their feelings and thoughts hidden, and I locked mine deep inside myself. Later on, I didn't want to confront the trauma I had suffered, and I had no idea how to start the healing process. I know now that hiding the actions of an abuser gives a child a higher risk of suffering from anxiety symptoms, depression, and the risk of suicide attempts. These psychological problems can disrupt a child's healthy development and have a lasting impact. Sexually abused children are often dysfunctional and distressed well into adulthood.

Perhaps if there had been someone who understood what was happening to me when I was a child and stopped the abuse, I might have begun to heal and not found it necessary to act out the trauma in my later years. My family didn't know how to deal with neither my sexual abuse nor the aftermath of it. My young life was shattered, and no one came to pick up the pieces.

Chapter II: Why Was This Still Happening to Me?

Cases of pedophilia and kidnappings dominated the news back in the 1980s, so there were constant feelings of fear while growing up as a child in Coventry. We lived in the inner city and terraced housing, and at the back was an alleyway in which myself and my neighbors would meet and play. We were all between the ages of four and eight. We would be scared away frequently when one of our older neighbors who was eighteen of age, would come out and flash us.

Growing up and becoming a teenager was challenging. I was developing physically and attracting the wrong sort of attention from the boys at my school. It reached a point where I seemed to be sexually harassed wherever I went—school, outside on the street, and at home by the relative, while the abuse continued.

When I stayed at a relative's house where the abuser lived, I was "allowed" to stay up late with him. He would put his hand inside my shirt and underwear as we sat on the couch. When I asked him about it, he replied, "This is how families show each other love."

"I don't see this happening anywhere else in my family, so why is this only happening to me?" I asked myself, feeling vulnerable and confused.

Anu Verma

The boys at school would push me up against the wall to grope me. They told me dirty jokes and said crude things. As a young woman, this caused me to feel even more unloved and to dislike myself.

"If the boys can grope me and have their way with me, then I am free to do whatever I like," this was my attitude toward life.

I misbehaved, and by the time I was sixteen, I was considered the black sheep of the family.

I have since been diagnosed as suffering from developmental trauma because of this abuse, which can affect healthy brain development — also emotional, physical, social, and cognitive performance. As a result of what was happening to me as a teenager, I had become more isolated from my family, and I began to stay out late with my friends.

I learned a strong work ethic when growing up, which remains the case today. My parents worked long hours, as most people from India do. By the time I was eleven years old, my job was to cook and clean for the entire family. Mum was working long hours, and Dad was doing long shifts at work. I was keeping up with my studies and having housework responsibilities.

My life retook a turn when, at the age of sixteen, I was sexually assaulted by an Asian college student. He was a big, strong guy, and a bully. He grabbed me, pushed me into an alley, and felt me up forcefully. I tried resisting him, though he was too strong as he had his hands around me. I remember stumbling home afterward, feeling used, vulnerable, and hurt. I had once again been damaged physically, emotionally, and mentally. I walked into my house, sobbing uncontrollably. I could see my mum through my tears, looking at me in alarm.

A family friend, who also attended my school, was present and shouted angrily at me. He said that it was my fault I was being molested. He explained how I had brought this upon myself because of the way I acted and dressed. He carried on saying that I was to blame, and I can remember thinking then that perhaps he was right.

I later found out that my family friend was bullied by this same gang and had feelings of hurt and anger. When there are no methods or ways to deal with these feelings of pain and sadness, it commonly comes out on those close to you, and on this unfortunate occasion, it was me.

Sadly, the student who assaulted me wasn't brought to justice, and I often wonder now how many other girls he may have molested. Sexual violence is prevalent in our society, and at the time, I didn't know how to find help. I didn't think that I could report the matter to the police or get therapy for myself. And here I was again, in a similar situation as before.

I received no sympathy when I struggled from the abuse or later on from the trauma that resulted, despite so many times when I longed for support. Nobody understood how or what they could do to support me, so it was easier to ignore me than to deal with these issues.

In retrospect, I now understand why I became so self-reliant. People saw me as independent throughout my life, though there is a vast difference between being independent and self-sufficient. I was forced to be self-sufficient, and I had to fight for myself.

The impact of sexual violence goes beyond physical injuries. The trauma of being sexually assaulted is all-consuming. It shatters you, leaving you ashamed, scared, and alone. Nightmares, flashbacks, and unpleasant memories plague you. Being attacked at sixteen heightened the memories I already had of being abused by Gary and my relative.

Continually thinking about all these traumatic incidents made me feel as if I was going crazy.

Anu Verma

I believed that I was "dirty" or "damaged goods." Relationships became a dangerous area, and depression a part of life. I kept seeing people who looked like my abuser. I felt that if I had been assaulted once in an alleyway, then it would happen again. I didn't trust men, and I thought no one would believe me if I dared to talk to them about it. Or they would say that it was my fault that this had happened, just like my family friend had told me that I had brought the abuse upon myself.

Between Sixteen and Eighteen Years of Age

I was determined to hold my head up and to have fun during my late teens. My best friend Monica and I would tell lies about where we were and what we were doing. Monica has always been a wonderful friend having my back during the rough times and the good. We would stay out late at night, which worried our families. We would tell our parents that we were at work, or I would say we were going to the library, while we had our clubbing clothes in our bags. I am sure that my parents suspected the truth, but I didn't care. I was angry with my family because they didn't seem to understand what I was going through.

The identity crisis I was suffering was again connected to my sexual abuse. Being an Asian brought up in the Western world, I felt like I was a victim, and I was mostly lost. There was always the confusion of the East and West cultures in which I was raised. We had a strong Eastern culture at home where we ate chapattis and curries, and I spoke Punjabi with my mum. I wore conservative western clothing, which never revealed much skin. Women cooked and cleaned while the men went out to work. At family gatherings, the men sat around and drank whiskey while the women would be in the kitchen, cooking and making sure the men were fed. My cousins would come around to visit, and we would sit upstairs and entertain ourselves. We were seen but not heard. We never had the supportive parenting that kids have these days. Life was survival. Our parents came into this country with nothing and so built everything from scratch. There were no boyfriends or girlfriends allowed, and even when kissing scenes would come on the TV, we would get shy and put our heads down. Communication wasn't great, and feelings were not discussed; it was 'tough' love.

Growing up as a teenager and going to school and being exposed to Western culture and how relaxed the English students were, would feel foreign to me. They were allowed out late, and their parents gave them so much freedom to speak, to be extroverts, whereas most Asian students seemed suppressed and, as a result, were more introverted.

To find my identity and place in my world, I began to bleach my hair blond. I wore so much fake tan that my skin looked orange, and my makeup was outrageous. Bright pink lipstick was my color of choice, and I thought I looked gorgeous. In reality, all of it was a total disaster. My friends teased me about how I dressed and the makeup I wore. I pretended not to care what people thought of me, but I wasn't happy. I hated everything about myself.

The United Kingdom has a long history of being influenced by distinct races and nationalities. It has created a diverse culture and economy, and some ethnic and racial discrimination is a fact of life. This external influence, together with my bizarre teenage behavior, made me a target for bullying and humiliation. What made it even worse was that I was trying to look as British as everyone else. Dyeing my hair and wearing heavy makeup made me feel as if I was part of the crowd. I was instead confused, as I refused to be honest with myself. I did not understand who I was.

Anu Verma

Chapter III: Wild and Crazy

When I was eighteen years old, I went to nightclubs with my friends. It was exciting to be a part of a crowd. The loud noise, lights, guys, and drinking alcohol impressed me. I was still comfort-eating, so I was carrying more weight than usual and wasn't feeling particularly great about myself. Going clubbing and drinking helped me to forget about reality, and I flirted with the men who were there because, for a moment, I felt as though I had power over them. This felt unusual, yet it was exciting.

Children, in general, have very little control over adult actions, and abused children have this flaunted and used against them with threats such as "I'll hurt your family if you say anything" or "Nobody will believe you if you tell them." My power had been taken away from me at a very young age when I was sexually molested. I was too young to consent to the men who took advantage of me, which led to me wanting to gain this power back when I was old enough to consent. Being intoxicated in nightclubs and being exposed to men gave me the perfect setting to do this. I was finally doing what I wanted, and I was having fun. However, I soon realized that I was fooling myself.

One particular night ended badly and left me yet again with a loss of self-esteem. I had gone to a club with a friend, and she invited her boyfriend and his friend to come along. This friend was an older man and was there to keep me company so I wouldn't be on my own in the club. I thought at first that this was a kind gesture, but I was wrong. All this man wanted to do was to kiss and touch me. It was awful. He was so much older than me, and I didn't like him. When I turned my head away to stop him from kissing me, he head-butted me. I fell over and had broken my nose. My nose didn't heal properly afterward, which caused me a lot of pain and suffering, which I eventually had to get surgically fixed. This was all because I had been afraid of getting myself into a situation where I might be abused again, and I had stood up for myself.

Nothing seemed to go right whatever I did! I had enjoyed myself, and it was the same again. Men assumed they could use me as a sexual toy, with no consideration for my feelings. I didn't even know this man's name, his background, or anything about him, except that he was the friend of a friend. I couldn't believe how many men had damaged my life by the time I was eighteen. I had been sexually abused, traumatized, molested, and physically assaulted. Being physically attacked by him was the final straw. I was determined to protect myself in any way that I could after that.

I had lost faith in men and just saw them as predators at this point in my life. I was desperate for my life to change. I had to do something drastic for that to change, and the simple answer was to find someone who loved me, so I started exploring my sexuality. I ventured out to see how it would be to be with a woman. I thought a woman wouldn't harm me as much as the men had. Women were kind and caring. This was a hard step for me to take, especially when telling my Mum because she refused to believe me. She shook her head sadly, and I knew then that I couldn't expect to receive any support from her.

Perhaps this decision was too drastic? I was still attracted to men, and so not surprisingly, my lesbian days didn't last long. I became a bisexual instead. This meant that I could look for a loving relationship with either a man or a woman. How I felt didn't matter to anybody by this time. Nobody seemed interested that I still regarded myself as unworthy of love or affection. I received no support or help, which I needed, and I was still confused by what had happened to me. My emotions were in turmoil. The feelings of hurt, pain, and confusion I had experienced when I was younger, became uppermost in my mind again. My self-worth had been damaged, I lacked self-esteem, I didn't value myself, and I felt like I had nothing to offer. I was damaged goods. All I could think of was that I had to find out who I was, to be able to heal and to have a much better life. The problem was that I didn't know how to go about this, and I began to experiment—trying different things while hoping to find something which would be the answer.

Chapter IV: My Dark Life

I moved to Manchester in 1998 to go to University. I wanted to study more in Biology as this was always a passion study, so following my passion would lead to a fulfilling career. My parents helped to fund my studies, which I am hugely grateful for. I also believed that getting away from Coventry would give me the freedom that I needed to sort out my feelings. The people who took advantage of me, until now, had played too significant a part in me losing my childhood innocence and the damage to my emotions. Once I was away; I might also escape from the demons, which always haunted me. It would be a fresh start, and I could live my own life. Unfortunately, I learned quickly that this would not be the case.

Manchester City was also struggling to find itself after the death of the textile and its other traditional industries. There were continual reports of stabbings, domestic violence, and back-alley sexual encounters. The Irish Republican Army had bombed it, then rebuilt and hosted the Commonwealth Games before witnessing years of rapid growth. The revolution which it had undergone had produced mixed results. Modern buildings stood next to traditional architecture, and the people seemed different compared to the people in Coventry. The cosmopolitan nature of the city, with its diverse cultures, opportunities, and fun, excited me, while the dangers simmering beneath the surface only made it more so.

Anu Verma

I had made some gay friends at University, and we loved Manchester and its nightlife. I lived in the student accommodations, and there was always so much going on with various groups I hung out with and at the multiple parties that I attended. Soon, I was sucked into a world of partying, drugs, and wild drinking sessions. My desire for women also became more prominent, so I could pursue my idea of being with a woman. I met many women, mainly in clubs as there were always so many opportunities in Manchester, being in such a diverse cultural city. I thought I had finally found myself, as a bisexual, but my desires went even further than this.

One evening I met Beth in a gay club. She was a gorgeous lady who was also a glamor model, and I went home with her. There were a lot of professional photographs scattered around her enormous house. She had a husband, Joel, and both wanted to introduce an element of fun into their marriage. I spent that night with Beth, and I felt safe when she touched me, but I couldn't let Joel do the same because of the previous situations I had been in with men. I could legally consent to have a sexual relationship. I was eighteen years old, and what we did was enjoyable. Even though we never saw each other again, I had found a new and exciting way to live. I was finally taking part in consensual and explorative sex, which felt so different from the sexual encounters I had been used to from such a young age. I was able to control what was taking place. This was no longer forced upon me. For this to take place provided a sense of freedom and a sense of liberation.

When I think about it now, I was taking a considerable risk. My friends were shocked and distressed when they learned how reckless I had become, but they didn't understand what was happening to me. I was still trying to escape from my old life, without knowing who I was, or what I ought to do. My wild behavior was destructive, and I soon felt very low about it. Why couldn't I just stop? I was struggling between the temporary feel-good at the moment vs. the after-effects. It was like a sugar high, which temporarily feels good, but then we are left feeling low and disappointed. The short-term high isn't worth the accompanying self-loathing. During my wild moments, I felt confident, I felt free, I felt happy, and that life was worth living as I was having so much fun. However, these wild moments were all alcohol and drug-fueled, and I was no longer suffering from the damages of the past. The pain had gone, and for these moments, I felt worthy.

I was confused in my late teens and early twenties. I understood nothing about relationships or how to respect my body, how to love myself, or how to give to others. I was utterly clueless. Relationships with men and women were very shallow as I just thought it involved me giving myself to them, and then that's it. It was heartless; I was not understood, and I did not understand people. My escape was losing myself by intoxication, and that's all I lived for at that time.

According to Dr. Amy Naugle, of the National Violence Against Women Prevention Research Center, being molested at a young age increases an individual's risk of experiencing major depressive episodes. At a rate of four times more than those who have not experienced molestation. These children feel isolated and need something to prove their worth. I was suffering from depression at the time. I was desperate too. Sexual assault, low self-esteem, and lack of identity had led to my wild behavior. I also had feelings of self-destruction, in which case, suicide had become my next adventure.

Suicide

My depressive symptoms were severe. They ranged from prolonged sadness to changes in my sleep pattern. I suffered from anger, agitation, and anxiety. I was pessimistic and indifferent. I thought about death a lot, including suicide. I felt guilty and worthless. I was crying out for love, and the true light within me to burn brighter. I knew that it could if the right person found me.

I often had thoughts of not being in my physical form and only existing in spirit. I could be free and float around as I pleased as a spirit, nobody would see me, and I would not have to be somebody I was not. I would not be stuck in an identity crisis as a spirit. I longed to reach this stage of my life sooner rather than later. This is how my thoughts of suicide arose. I would get these thoughts usually when I was intoxicated or when I felt lonely. There were a few incidents throughout my years at University when we would go to clubs, and I would drink too much and then take more drugs than my body could tolerate, and I would end up a mess on the floor and be escorted home or to the hospital. These nights of destruction raised concerns amongst my friends though nobody understood or knew what was going on with me. I never even understood what was happening to me, why I was feeling these dark thoughts, and why I was self-destructing to the point of death.

I was into the late 90s trance and techno-culture, and so I loved attending festivals which played this music. Being at festivals, I felt so free, and I hadn't experienced as much fun as I did when I was at a festival, whether for one day or three staying in a tent. I had a habit of leaving my friends just to be by myself. My friends worried about me going off for hours on end though I was having the time of my life, absorbing the atmosphere, the music, the freedom, I felt carefree. It was great.

At one particular festival in Liverpool, it ended up the opposite of 'great' as I awoke in casualty. What had happened was that I met a group of lads and we were laughing and joking and one of them, a nice chap, bought me a drink. All I could recall was drinking and then finding myself waking up with four doctors and nurses above me trying to gain my consciousness. I had collapsed in the dance tent because whatever drug the 'nice' chap placed in my drink had an adverse effect on me, and then apparently, a festival ambulance was called to take me into the casualty tent. There was no sign of these chaps or my friends. I was all alone trying to recuperate from this toxic substance.

"It happens a lot," the nurse explained.

"Isn't there anything you can do?" I asked.

VICTIM 2 VICTOR

"Well. We always advise girls not to accept drinks from strangers," she shrugged.

It struck me how it was my fault for taking the drink—not the man's fault for drugging me.

"Do you know if anything else happened to me?" I asked, rather worriedly.

She looked down at her shoes, "I don't know, sweetheart, it's not a yes, but it's not a no either" She didn't know, and I never would know if I had been taken advantage of or not.

I could only wish that nothing terrible had happened. After some rest and a cup of tea, I was free to leave the casualty tent and find my friends to reunite with them and to forget about what had happened.

Even though I was out at clubs or festivals, I didn't actively seek to end my life; the danger of the substances could have ended my life very easily. I had some incidents where I actively attempted to end my life. One particular incident was when my friend and I were invited to an after-club party. The party was in a block of flats, it was a tall building of forty floors, and there was a balcony where a few others were talking, and the music was blasting. I had drunk a lot and was under the influence of drugs and was feeling low. I knew that alcohol was a depressant for me; it always was; therefore, why I took drugs to help counteract this depressiveness. On this particular night, the drugs never worked, and I was feeling lower than ever. I wanted to end this feeling and for the sadness to go away, and I wished I did not have to live longer because my life was a mess. I felt that I would never get better, I would always fail, and I would always lose. These dark thoughts dominated my mind, and I went up to the balcony and went climbing over the top to jump off, and hopefully, I could fly away into the darkness, and nobody would ever see me or my irrelevance in this world. My friend had caught me and screamed at me to stop then came running to pull me down. "What are you doing?" she shouted at me.

Anu Verma

I was in a daze and just shrug at her, "I have no idea, Shaz, thanks for saving me. Let's go and party."

My attitude to these attempts was very blasé, and because of this lack of care, my friends never really had much to say and so shrugged it off. This was the same during my club incidents and ending up in casualty at the hospital. I could never really explain why I did anything, and maybe this was due to my lack of communication skills growing up and the suppression that I suffered. Communicating my feelings would always remain an issue in my life until I sought help and found a better way.

The next time my attempt at suicide happened, I was staying in Gran Canaria with friends. I climbed onto a second-story balcony and over the railing, getting ready to jump. My friends shouted and screamed at me to stop until they finally managed to drag me backward to safety. They were horrified that I had tried to end my life. Confused, and frightened too, that I would try again. They tried their best to persuade me to stop thinking about it. I remember shrugging off their concerns as if it didn't matter, but I still bear the scars on my stomach from where they pulled me off the railings that day. They were rough with me in their haste to save my life, and it's something I will never forget.

My third desire to end my life occurred when I had entered into an abusive relationship, so all the dark thoughts had come back to me. I had again lost my feelings of self-worth, lost my power and my self-respect. I was walking along a busy street with my partner at the time. Cars speeding past were too much of a temptation. I walked along this busy road hoping to get hit, but then I was pulled back by him. I was unsure why he saved me because his intentions for me weren't healthy. He asked me repeatedly what I thought I was doing, and I laughed. I realized that I must have seemed unconcerned to him, but these dark thoughts ruled my mind. I don't think I completely lost this feeling, but things began to happen then, which made me realize that being alive might not be as bad as I thought.

VICTIM 2 VICTOR

The Bar Life

I began working full time in a bar where I quickly became the supervisor. I felt on top of the world because I had been promoted. Somebody had finally believed in my abilities and had entrusted me with additional responsibilities. I never knew I had it in me to reach a position of authority. I never realized how important control was in my life, the ability to make choices, even if I make the wrong choices. Given all of this responsibility and freedom, I struggled, and my behavior once again became manic. I threw the craziest parties at the bar while the boss was away. I treated my customers to free drinks. My name was linked to partying and having a good time. While I was doing this, I also had classes to attend at University, and there were days when I was so hungover that I couldn't get out of bed. My bar gig was paying good money. I had made new "friends," but after a while, I couldn't help questioning whether this was the life that I wanted or the career I could have for the rest of my life. I was working forty hours per week and still attending University. I wasn't studying as much as I should have. I was busy and never minded the parties which went on until late.

I was eventually sacked from this role as the owner had seen the CCTV footage of the parties that I was throwing while she was away. She simply called me and said, "I've seen the video, and you are not welcome here anymore," so that was the end of the bar work.

Fortunately, I had saved my wages, and I began instead to study harder, so maybe being sacked was a blessing. I went to classes intending to graduate. If I could graduate, then I promised myself a trip around the world. I could travel for six months before settling down to my career. This decision made me feel as if I had finally got my act together. In the end, my around the world adventure in six months turned into sixteen months of pure excitement and escape.

Chapter V: Traveling

My life in Manchester was fun and dark at the same time. The fun parts were the parties, great friends that I had, and the endless fun. The dark times were when drugs and alcohol were involved. I wanted to get away from this darkness, and the only way I felt I could achieve this was to leave Manchester. I had saved up enough money through my bar job to buy an around the world ticket. I felt so excited as I was set with my travel route planner, and we planned where I would go and what I would see. This felt like freedom, and I was so looking forward to escaping. I had a few friends who wanted to join me though I needed to travel alone with no ties and with nobody to dictate where I would go or how long I would stay anywhere.

Traveling made me feel as if I had escaped the demons and pressures of a destructive life. I didn't plan where I was going or book anywhere to stay. I would arrive and look in my planner guide to find a place to put my luggage and sleep. It felt amazing to be living like this. I didn't mind having to wait around for visas. I would work and travel, and the money which I had earned would help to fund and prolong my journey. I enjoyed where I was until it was time to start traveling again. There was so much to do and explore everywhere I went. I loved my new life. I never actually followed the route that I had planned with my Travel planner as I was too freestyle. What was meant to be a six-month trip ended up being sixteen months.

My journey started in America, and I traveled some more after that. I worked in Sydney and Moura, in Australia, experiencing the Aussie life along the east and west coasts. I was happy and free because I focused on the exciting time that I was having. It made me forget about the demons at the back of my mind.

Australia

When I had been in Australia for a year, I traveled on a backpacker bus from Cairns in the north along the east coast. It took a group of us to all the small towns, and I experienced the authentic Aussie culture. I was awarded a scuba diving qualification in the Great Barrier Reef, and I became obsessed with underwater life. Someone told me that the Great Barrier Reef was the largest living organism in the world. It looked so otherworldly when I saw it that I fell in love with being there. To complete this part of my adventure, I sky-jumped 15,000 feet above the reef, in Cairns, which made me feel freer and more alive than I had ever been. I longed for extreme high-risk sports during my travels, maybe because they resembled how I was feeling, and it hadn't been that long since my suicidal attempts. These near-death thrills appealed a lot to me during these times. They reminded me that I was alive. I enjoyed the brush with death, and I liked the control that it gave me as it put the choice in my hands.

Three months later, I was in Sydney. I found a daytime telesales job and an evening telemarketing job. These jobs provided the money I needed to carry on enjoying my Aussie experience. I took up swimming to keep in shape, and I stayed in a hostel with some backpacking friends. They were employed in various roles, from fruit picking to carpentry. We eventually found a house in Woolloomooloo, and the six of us partied as often as we could. We were determined to have fun. There was a pub nearby, and we took advantage of the events. My Australian visa allowed me to travel for one year, but my work visa was only three months. I planned to go to Melbourne when this visa expired. So, I left my backpacking friends behind and caught the train. When I arrived in Melbourne, I went on a Neighbors Tour, and I met some actors, and we had a great night drinking with them. I booked on to the 'Oz Experience' tour up the west coast of Oz. This green bus is the most cost-effective and convenient way for a backpacker to travel around Oz, and you get to meet lots of other backpackers. I spent Christmas having a barbecue on the beach and took a trip into the Australian Outback to visit Ayers Rock, a massive sandstone monolith in the middle of nowhere. It isn't surprising that this is a national monument, but the heat was unbearable at fifty degrees centigrade. I struggled with this. All I wanted to do was to jump in a pool to cool off.

On New Year's Day, I took a train to Perth. It was a long journey, and, in the end, I celebrated on the train with other travelers whom I had just met. The trip was a magical experience, and I couldn't remember having felt happier. I joined an employment agency in Perth, hoping to find bar work in the Outback. I got a job in Moora, a small town in Western Australia with around two thousand people. I experienced a lot of indigenous cultures here, which mainly revolved around drinking alcohol. They were a very relaxed culture that I respected, and it was nice to be away from the rat race and fast-paced life. I also learned about sheep shearing. It was fun!

Despite my confusion in my sexuality, I found myself a biker boyfriend called Jonno. He had a history of dating the girls who came to work in the pub. I had a room in the hotel next to it, and Jonno waited outside my window with flowers. Just like Romeo! When he asked me to be his girlfriend, it was so sweet, although I did feel a little embarrassed at the time. Jonno worked in the city, and I hung out with the locals when he left Moora. We often used to party all night. It was the first time I had felt special. Jonno did little things that made me realize that not all men were bad, like when he bought me flowers and cooked for me, and he used to take me on bike rides to various spots around the town. Although we both knew that I was only here for a short time, Jonno never made me feel sad, and he never made me feel that I wasn't worthy. Jonno showed me that relationships could be happy. I just didn't think that any man would want me to be their girlfriend. There is a vast difference between how this made me feel and the shame that I had previously felt when I was being taken advantage of by a man. This wasn't a destructive relationship. Looking back now, I can see how he impacted my way of thinking.

Fortunately, the owners of the pub took care of me and made sure that I was safe. I felt privileged to be with them and treated as a member of their family. Apart from accommodation and food, they paid me another three thousand dollars when my three months were up. This meant that I had enough money for several more months of travel. I was so excited that I could continue my journey. Jonno drove me back to Perth, where we spent a few days together. It was good but also the end of our relationship. We both knew that it wouldn't last. I was a backpacker, and so was not there to stay. I was also still very new to relationships and hadn't quite figured out if I was more into men or women at this stage of my life. It had always been my intention to move on. Jonno taught me that not all men are bad. He was genuine and romantic, so I feel that he was sent to me to give me some light into my darkness and my feelings towards men. He did impact my way of thinking, and I thank him dearly for this.

During the last part of my stay in Australia, I traveled along the West Coast, visiting some impressive towns, and saw some fantastic sights. Everything seemed great until I stayed in a dormitory that I will never forget. One of the bad things about the backpacker lifestyle was the bed bugs. They were awful. This one was infested with them. I can remember packing all of my stuff at four o'clock in the morning after I had seen these little black bugs crawling around my mattress, trying to infest my backpack, clothes, and sleeping bag. I had to go! I suppose it was something I should have expected. So many backpackers used them every day, and there were bound to be some unhygienic travelers. Also, given how hot and humid it was in Australia, the infestations could easily hibernate and reproduce. It was the perfect place for them.

Anu Verma

New Zealand

I booked my flight out of Australia to New Zealand. I wanted to visit both the north and south islands. New Zealand was known for its extraordinary scenery, ranging from lofty mountains to impressive underground cave systems and roaring rivers. There were vast glaciers, boiling hot springs, and incredible golden sand beaches along its rugged coastlines. It had the coolest cities, hidden spots, and incredible wildlife. I thought that New Zealand was magical. Being in nature and the wonders of the country, I feel, had a significant impact on my healing. Connecting with nature does have tremendous effects on mental health, and so I think that by me being here had started to repair my brokenness.

By the time I had gone to most of the places I wanted to visit, I felt that I had fallen into the authentic Kiwi experience. It's believed to be the place where bungee jumping was invented, so of course, I had to try this even though it was an extreme sport. One of the highest bungee jumps you could do began above the raging waters of the Nevis River in Queenstown. It wasn't for the faint-hearted, as it's from one hundred and thirty-four meters above the river. I was also excited about trying white water rafting, even after learning it was the scariest in the world. I am glad that I experienced this. The adrenaline pumping through my veins reminded me of when I was about to jump off those buildings in my attempt to end my life. The feelings I experienced were of danger and freedom at the same time. The experience was exhilarating, but my manic behavior could have cost me my life. There was a clear difference between the adrenaline in a controlled, safe situation versus the adrenaline released from when I was trying to end my life. In retrospect, this difference signaled a change in me. I could either be the creator of my own life and experience more of the wonders of the world, or I could destroy my life and end it without truly having experienced happiness and freedom; it was my choice.

I went with a group of friends on a white-water rafting trip. It felt like being in paradise as we ran the grade five rivers, but it meant that I was taking part in yet another extreme sport. I often ended up under the raft and made my way back to the surface, laughing and spluttering. However, on one adventure, things became a little more frightening. The trip was okay, to begin with, but as we were running the rapids, I went into the water. Unfortunately, I lost my contact lenses, and I almost drowned. While it was happening, I couldn't stop thinking about the sixty or more people who had lost their lives while white water rafting in New Zealand, and I was frightened. When I was underwater, it was as if my life was ebbing away from me. As I counted the seconds and tried to claw my way to the top, the waves were against me. They kept on pushing me deeper under the water. If that wasn't bad enough, the instructor had to turn the raft the right way up to make it safely through the rapids. He jumped on one end of it, in an attempt to do so, but which meant I was pushed deeper into the water. I nearly lost consciousness, but Heaven must have helped me. I came up just in time to catch my breath.

I did wonder afterward what I had been doing in level five rapids. They were the most turbulent and dangerous torrents in the world, but I am still glad to this day that I took part in both of these extreme sports. Apart from the last incident, it was a wonderful experience!

This experience was a life-changer for me because it made me realize that I wanted to live. I wanted to experience more and to travel more and to see more. This was the point when I started to appreciate life more and the beauties of it. Life wasn't all about doom and gloom; there was so much more that I was about to witness. This is a beautiful world that we live in, it is full of wonders, and I wanted to see it all. This is why I can happily say that traveling helped to heal me and to reform and reshape my views and beliefs. I was sent on this journey overseas to overcome the dark thoughts and oversee these feelings with love and light and happiness. This is why I was so heavily drawn to Buddhism, the monasteries and temples of which I will discuss more later on in this book.

I also enjoyed watching a traditional Maori dance in New Zealand and traveling around the country. My only complaint about the

Anu Verma

Maori people was that I had ham in my veggie sandwiches! They couldn't understand that I was a vegetarian or what this meant, and they wouldn't give me vegetables to eat by themselves. I still thought they were delightful people, and I enjoyed my visit.

After spending thirteen months in Australia and New Zealand during 2002 and 2003, I went on a further three-month journey to South East Asia. I traveled to Thailand, Cambodia, Laos, and Vietnam. I wanted to do everything again that might be adventurous or would help me to learn about the country which I was visiting. I toured around, and I saw the white, sandy beaches of Thailand. The ancient temples of Cambodia. I enjoyed the unassuming charm, and beauty, of Laos. Also, the many famous and historical sites in Vietnam.

Cambodia

My visit to Cambodia was a surreal experience. I went to the sad place where all the skulls of those who had died in the genocide, committed by the former Khmer Rouge government, were on display behind glass. The Museum is in a Phnom Penh high school, formerly used as a torture center and prison. Although the Cambodians themselves seemed to be proud of their history and remnants of this violent past, it felt disturbing and upsetting. Seeing all the vestiges of innocent people murdered for no reason other than selfishness and greed, I sat in complete silence with tears welling up in my eyes while I was back in my room in Pnom Penh. I thought about how lucky I was to be given the gift of life. How lucky I was to be born in England, which was a developed country and where the economy was booming, and options were at our hands. I was, at this point, unsure as to why I had wanted to end my life. My parents had moved to the UK for a better life for them and their children, so why was I allowing the past events of my life to destroy their dreams? I was blown away by the human ability to forgive and to move on. The genocide took place not so long ago, yet people had pulled their lives together after such traumatic experiences. It struck me seeing so much beauty being born from something so ugly. How can people use the past as a measure of their growth? Cambodia changed my perspective about life, and I could say that I became more grateful and appreciative of the wonders of life. The images of the skulls would remain with me for the rest of my life. I needed this. God sent me here for this purpose, and I have been forever grateful to have been given this opportunity to travel and to see the world during the times that I most needed it.

Thailand

I discovered that I loved Thailand the most out of all the places I visited in 2002. It was a diverse country with beautiful beaches and crystal blue waters. The food was delicious, and the people were friendly. They always seemed to smile and were polite. If anyone were in trouble, they would help them, and they also translated what they said if someone didn't speak Thai. Maybe this is why Thailand is called the "Land of Smiles." It was such a beautiful place!

It was also exciting to learn about Thai culture and Buddhism. I enjoyed spending time with the monks in the monasteries. I knew about their simple ways, how meditation was a way of life, and how they only ate one meal a day. The monks used to get up at three o'clock in the morning to meditate. They then rested and taught during the day, so they didn't need a lot of physical energy. Everything was peaceful, and I very much admired their contentment. I was told that Thailand was the perfect place to learn the complexities of Buddhism and that it was traditional for a Thai man to become a monk in his life. Temples were sacred, and it was forbidden to do anything on its property, which might be unwholesome. At the monastery I went to, seated and walking meditations were taking place. Along with Dhamma talks and you could meet the Buddhist instructors. I learned that some monasteries asked their visitors to perform daily chores, chant with them, and follow their rules.

Buddhism has always been a religion close to my heart; I cannot say why because I feel that my love comes from deep inside. Maybe from a past life? Perhaps it was the monks and their simple and peaceful way of living and one which I respect so much. Some of my Buddhist teachings include giving generously to others, to free ourselves from attachments, to take the journey within to seek answers, to be here now, to release feelings of hate, resentment, and fear, and that we are the writers of our destiny. It took me many years to practice many of these teachings, though I was on a journey of enlightenment, and that's all that mattered to me. Buddhism gave me the hope of a fulfilling life, a life free of hurt, and a life worth living. I was still traveling and escaping and seeking answers externally, and I thought my answers lay in Thailand. It took me years to meditate appropriately to find answers from within my soul, and so I can write this book now and share my journey with you.

I took an overnight bus from Bangkok to the South Islands. I swallowed a sleeping pill to help me fall asleep on the bus. When I woke up at the end of the journey, I discovered that my backpack had been tampered with, and some of my money had been stolen. I was frightened. My luggage was under my seat, and I had thought, was out of sight. When I was on another bus in Thailand, I discovered that my backpack had been opened. It was stored underneath along with the other bags, and someone had put a bottle of vodka inside it. The drivers were supposed to be trustworthy. They transported all the backpackers through Thailand, but I soon discovered that some of them took advantage of this role by robbing us while we slept. This ignited my feelings of vulnerability and being taken advantage of, and so I felt uneasy and that I wasn't safe.

Bangkok was a great cultural experience, but I was excited to be in the South Island of Koh Tao. I was staying in a bungalow. Thank heavens, there weren't any dormitories or bed bugs. I could have my space and to sleep when I wanted to. I loved visiting the Thai temples and the islands, also the taste of the local dishes. Green and massaman curries with sticky rice and the mango and rice dishes. One of my favorite desserts soon became coconut milk pudding, but the place I loved best in Thailand was Pai. It was in the northern mountains. To get to Pai, I traveled through the city of Chiang Mai, which is in the same area, and home for hundreds of elaborate Buddhist temples. The fifteenth-century Wat Chedi Luang was

VICTIM 2 VICTOR

covered in carved serpents. Chiang Mai was a bustling city, filled with tourists and workers from all over the world. There were many places where you could work remotely on the internet if you needed to earn money as a freelancer, but I just wanted to travel and meditate.

After a while, I visited the south and its many spectacular islands. It was a great place to relax and to socialize with the other backpackers. I met a lot of different people and learned about their cultures. I enjoyed myself immensely. I met Andrea, who was a nurse from Australia. We had a full moon party at Koh Phangan, but I remember little about that. The Full Moon Party is an all-night beach party that originated in Hat Rin on Ko Phangan, Thailand, in 1985. The party takes place on the night of, before, or after every full moon. Tourists mostly attend it.

A few of us, including Andrea and myself, hit the vodka Redbull buckets. I am still not sure what was in them. The next thing I knew, I was waking up on the beach, watching an incredible sunrise, and I couldn't find my camera. I felt exhausted. Someone said later that amphetamines were commonly put into buckets to spike the partygoers to make them an easy target to be mugged. I wasn't sure if I had lost my camera, or if someone had stolen it. I couldn't remember what had happened to it, or anything else. I do, however, remember meeting a guy who said that he was not a bisexual, but a tri-sexual. He was one of the thousands of crazy people who were on the beach that night.

When I woke up, I felt happy, unlike the incidents when I was spiked and taken advantage of. This time in Thailand, it felt different. I was with a group of travelers whom I trusted and whom I knew had my back, and so I never felt vulnerable. This was the way when meeting other travelers and the law of familiarity; we were all in a foreign country together, so we trusted each other.

I walked into the sea with them the next morning, not realizing that it probably wasn't the most hygienic thing to do. Many partygoers had urinated in the water using it as a toilet while we had been there.

Anu Verma

The stench was awful. Luckily, the boats arrived that morning to take us back to the islands where we were staying. My friends and I finally located a boat going back to ours. The others in my party went to their rooms to get some sleep, but I found it challenging to do this during the day. So, I packed up and left for the next island, Koh Lanta, where I rested and recuperated.

Laos

I still had more traveling to do and had been looking forward to visiting Laos. It was a long journey overland to get there. I went by bus because of my tight budget and sense of adventure. Using my planner guides, I wanted to retrace my steps. I was going back to Bangkok, Chiang Mai, and Pai before reaching the Laos border. My visa arrived a few days after I gave my passport to a local travel agency, but I didn't mind waiting. I enjoyed walking around Chiang Mai, meeting people, and taking the free classes. I took a cookery course and attended another class where I was taught massage therapy. Crossing the border into Laos was an experience! I had traveled by bus to get there, and it was inspected by the military every few hours.

I made friends in Laos and even taught English to the inspectors and guards. It was often called a "forgotten country" as tourists tended not to go there. It was dirty, but also an underdeveloped country. I thought it was perfect for relaxing and chilling out. The villages and cities moved slowly, and I didn't see many people on the streets in the early morning. There also weren't any advertisements for busy places. I went on a longboat while I was there, which ended up being an uncomfortable trip. A transvestite guided us down the river. She had quite a unique image. Her face was masked with white makeup, and she wore bright lipstick and blue eyeshadow; it was a very profound look. I found myself wondering how she managed to stay like that in the heat and humidity of the jungle.

Laos had a mountainous landscape, which was stunning, and had ancient cultural attractions. There was an old-world feel to it. The people were friendly, and again, there were a lot of Buddhist temples. I thought it was a breathtaking place, relatively untouched by tourism. I visited That Luang, a national symbol and the most sacred monument in the country. It looked like a fortress surrounded by high walls, with its two temples and impressive forty-five-meter-high stupa covered in gold leaf on the top.

Finally, it was time to book my return flight to the United Kingdom. After sixteen months of traveling and being away from home, I needed to get back and restart my life. I cried at the airport as I sat in my T-shirt and Thai pants, which I had bought on Koh San Road in Bangkok. I will never forget my travels through those beautiful places. I had been mostly free of the demons which haunted me from when I was in the United Kingdom. The experience had made me realize that I needed to finish my further education as quickly as possible and to start a career. I needed to find my career path and have a stable income, which would help to fund further travels as I was now obsessed with traveling. I had so many more places which I longed to visit. It excited me at the thought of having a stable income would then allow me to achieve peace, calmness, and control over my life and destiny.

Anu Verma

Chapter VI: Returning to the UK

I looked different when I stepped off the plane in the United Kingdom. I had a dark tan and short hair, which was almost like a boy cut. I had gained some weight and was chubby. My parents didn't recognize me at the airport when they came to pick me up. It was funny watching them look for me. I don't know what they were expecting, but after being away for such a long time, it didn't seem strange that my appearance had changed. I felt more at peace with myself when I returned from my travels. I wasn't wearing make-up, I never bleached my hair, I wore simple clothes. I wasn't trying to be somebody who I was not. The impact that traveling had on me was the best impact I had ever had, until this point, at twenty-three. Traveling was my godsend. Trying to get my life into order before leaving Thailand, I had accepted a place at the University of Essex to study for a master's degree in Sports Science. I had no idea what I wanted to pursue in my career, all I knew was that I enjoyed Biology and Physiology, and this master's degree contained all the modules that I would enjoy learning. Although it was only June, I was ready to start in September. This gave me a few months to work and to save some money.

Being back in England, my free-spirited and relaxed nature made me feel like an outsider. After my travels, I didn't know how to dress, and I must have looked like a hippie. I wore baggy Thai pants, which I bought from Koh San Road, a famous road for tourists in the City of Bangkok. I wore one-dollar flip flops, which I purchased from Vietnam, along with cheap vest tops. I decided that it was time to change. I wanted to try again to fit into the culture that I had been away from for so long, and gaining my Master's Degree at Essex University was one of the hardest things I had ever attempted. I spent long hours researching journals to compare studies carried out by researchers. I had to do this for my essays, dissertations, and thesis. I had been shortsighted for a long time, and the extra screen time on my computer made my eyesight a lot worse. However, it didn't stop me from taking driving lessons and finally gaining my driver's license.

Canada

After graduation, I traveled to Canada to gain work experience and to learn more about cardiac rehabilitation. It was part of the therapy which optimized physical function in patients who had cardiac disease or who had recently undergone surgery.

To support me, I took a job in a fitness studio where it was possible to use my work visa. I stayed in Ottawa, in a room which I rented from a charming landlord. One day as I was walking home, I passed a laser eye treatment center, and I realized that they might correct my vision. I went through the procedure and was by myself while I was recovering. That was me, Miss Independent! I had learned a long time ago that I needed to be a fighter to survive, and I was also determined to be a victor. I finally gained a twenty-twenty vision, and I ditched my glasses and contact lenses. Once my eyesight had settled down again, I felt as if a miracle had occurred. I am still thankful for it today. I felt so relieved that it could rectify my defects. I was not a total failure, after all.

I felt confident in my skills in cardiac rehabilitation, and with the added experience in Canada, I was optimistic that I was about to find my career. That was until I worked in a hospital. I had no idea that this environment wouldn't be right for me. Perhaps it was the smell, patients' demands, or the chaos? I even tried working in the laboratories, but it still wasn't for me. I was too much of an extrovert. I needed to be around people.

Anu Verma

Spending my Earnings

I returned to the UK once my work experience in Canada had ended. After some job searching, I had ventured into medical sales as my career of choice as it gave me the flexibility to travel and plan my diary. I also got a company car, mobile phone, and a laptop. So, there I was, working long hours in medical sales during the day and tutoring in the evenings and the weekends. Even though I was not backpacking, I was again in flight-mode and living off adrenaline. I was also not having to deal with the trauma and abuse that was still profoundly haunting me. I already had bought my first ever apartment in Manchester though I always wanted to make more money and purchase another property. One property was not enough for me; one job was not enough for me; a relationship at this point in my life wasn't enough for me. I needed more of everything. A case of greed had kicked in.

Being a typical university graduate in her mid-twenties, I didn't have a lot of experience managing my finances. I thought if I had money in the bank, I was okay, so I went crazy! I bought a Mercedes SLK convertible and put thousands of pounds down as a deposit on an off-plan property in Dubai. This meant that it still had to be built. They marketed it as an excellent investment, with a promise that I could become rich. Unfortunately, I had invested at the wrong time. A recession put a stop to the building work, and many people lost their money. I lost everything that I had invested.

Although my car was gorgeous, it was a depreciating asset. So, I also lost thousands of pounds on this. The fantastic feeling of having a great new car and money in the bank, didn't last. As my bank account emptied, I found myself sinking into depression. It felt like my self-esteem had dropped to the bottom of a well, but this experience had taught me a lot about finance. I would, in the future, need to be careful about what I did with my money and not make impulsive purchases. My feeling of being on 'top of the world' linked to my self-worth and to the perception of what others could see and to what I could show. When this didn't work, I wanted to make myself feel better, so I looked for a relationship.

Anu Verma

Chapter VII: My Life Is Like a Never-Ending Circle

Until then, my focus had been working and making money. I had taken up running and was running in half marathons, which were great for my mental state of mind. I was attending the gym regularly though I was still not in the best of shape as I wasn't eating great and was over-indulging on carbohydrates, chocolates, and cakes. I was looking for something. I was hungry for something, and I was filling this hunger with food. There hadn't been time for a partner or a relationship. So, I decided to test the waters, and I tried online dating.

Most of my chats fizzled out. Most dates were looking for a fun-time girl, which I didn't have any desire to be. I started speaking to a guy named Dean, who claimed he was a recruiter. Whether he was or wasn't remains a mystery. It was 2007, and we didn't have all the online facilities we do now to look up people. LinkedIn didn't exist, and Facebook had just been launched. I met Dean as he seemed like a great guy. We chatted over drinks, and it was pleasant. When we had dinner, I excused myself and went to the toilet. When I came back, we talked more about our lives and getting to know each other as you do on a first date. All I remembered after that was waking up naked at his place the next morning.

It was a complete shock! How had I got there? What happened? Did I consent to any of it? I asked Dean, and he laughed. He told me I was drunk the night before. I thanked him for a great evening, still somewhat confused. He cooked me breakfast, and he seemed like the nicest guy on earth. But I was still a little perplexed. I was sure that I only had two drinks.

I felt vulnerable as I was getting dressed, and I ordered a taxi home. We continued texting as usual. I didn't suspect that anything was wrong with him, or his explanation about our first night. I blamed myself for getting drunk, and we met the next weekend. We went to a club this time where we drank vodka and danced like all the other couples who were having a great time. We must have consumed more on this second date, and I could vaguely remember getting into a taxi with him. But that was all. Everything was a complete blank after that. I woke up next to him in my bed the following morning. I was naked and in total shock. I didn't know how I had got home, undressed, or into bed. I blamed myself again for drinking too much.

I told myself that I needed to stop drinking. The blackouts I had experienced with this guy were as scary as hell, and not safe. The only other times I had experienced these blackouts were when I had overdosed on alcohol and drugs at night clubs while I was at University, and I was sent to casualty though that was eight years ago, and I had not touched drugs since those dark nights. When Dean left, I looked in the mirror. I felt ashamed, used, and violated. I was very sore down below, and I didn't have any idea why.

This time he didn't text to thank me for the glorious night we had, and when I texted him, he ignored me. As the day went on, I felt even more upset at the thought of being used. I left my apartment and headed to the pharmacy to get some cream for the soreness that I was experiencing. I had read about my symptoms, and it sounded as if I was suffering from thrush. I was furious about this, and I told him in a text that afternoon. I was quietly hoping that he was suffering as much as I was.

I asked my best friend what she thought I should do about the thrush, and also my blackouts. She was angry and wanted to know if I had left my drinks with him during the evening. I said that I had done when I excused myself to go to the toilet. He had full control of those drinks, and he also bought me the drinks. My friend advised me to seek help and go to a doctor immediately for a test. She thought they had drugged me since a few drinks by themselves shouldn't have caused blackouts. I did as she advised, and I went to a walk-in center and explained to them I had a blackout the previous night, and the week before, the same happened and with the same guy. It was apparent to the nurse what had happened. It was also evident to me though I was in a major case of denial. I was vulnerable, and I felt like a victim as I held my head down, feeling violated. I had the same tests that were given to rape victims. The results came back positive. The evidence was undeniable. I had been drugged and raped.

The nurse discussed the possibilities of taking this further with the police as the perpetrator would be arrested, and this case could go to the courts. If I had been the strong woman I am today, I would have pressed charges, and justice would have been served. Unfortunately, at that time in my life, I didn't have the power or the strength to put up a fight. I was still damaged emotionally from the previous incidents in which I had been involved. I didn't know how to deal with the hurt or how to begin to heal myself from the trauma of date rape. So, I decided not to do anything about it. I let him get away with a malicious act, not only once, but twice.

Not reporting rape has become a widespread problem amongst women. One victim was asked if she had been raped, and why didn't she report it? Her answer was, "Why would I report it?". The problem with date and drug rape is that often, no one believes the victim. The investigation, court case, and continually being asked questions can make taking a man to court almost as painful as the actual rape. I felt just like that other victim did when she said, "Why would I report it?"

But that wasn't the end of it! I missed my period the following month. The nurse at the clinic gave me a pregnancy test, and the truth was there on the testing stick. I was pregnant, and I became depressed. I wanted to deal with it by getting rid of the pregnancy. I just needed to get on with my life and pretend that nothing had happened. I desperately tried to ignore the situation.

My good friend Izabelle helped me when I ended the pregnancy. I had taken the pill option and can still vividly remember how horrific it was. The contractions caused by the pill were an experience like no other. They were excruciatingly painful. As I was going through them, I thought giving birth to a baby might also be painful, but not like this. That would be a magical time. To have those contractions for the baby of a rapist made them feel like the deadliest experience in the world. I suffered physically and mentally from the abortion.

Rape, especially if there is a pregnancy, is invasive and traumatic. Victims of drug rape are at risk of having mental health issues. I found ways to cope and to escape from this pain. My vice, which I turned to was work. I worked more, so I did not have to face going home. I kept myself busy and preoccupied and found that the sadness struck me during my car journeys to and from work when I was alone. This was the time that I had to reflect on what I was going through. I often cried in the car, bursting out and wailing and hoping no other driver would look at me. Rape does not go away. It can stay with the victim for many years, and receiving treatment is vital.

The abortion brought to the surface more of my guilt and anger, which I had been hiding. I suffered again from further trauma. I couldn't look at myself in the mirror. My depression often brought me to my knees, in tears, and feelings of guilt. I realized that I had to make some changes in my life. So, I made a deal with myself to place all of my energy and focus on building my business. Working every hour of every day would help me escape from the horrible emotions.

Another Rollercoaster

I continued to place my efforts and energies by establishing myself with my tutoring business. I was also training to run the full marathon, which took up a significant investment of my time.

Anu Verma

Looking back now, I can see that I still had so much learning to do about myself and others. I had massive defenses up and did not trust anybody. I did not know how to give my time or energy to others due to a fear of getting hurt and betrayed again. I went from one failed relationship to another because this was all I knew. I never understood the vital elements of a relationship or how to make them work. I still never knew how to love myself. My escape was my work.

Lost and weak, I felt that I needed a man in my life. So, I began a new relationship with a colleague, Alex, who was more like a father figure than a boyfriend. I thought I could look up to him for protection because this is what I was craving right now. I was looking for somebody to protect me and to comfort me because I felt so damaged and so broken. He was six feet tall and had a fabulous physique. Little did I know that he also came with his baggage and demons.

Alex was an alcoholic. He could drink three liters of straight vodka in one night. He would drink anything alcoholic in my apartment. He was codependent on alcohol, and I became his lifeline. Our relationship continued for a year, but I knew that being with him wasn't right for me. He was always drunk and wouldn't step up to his responsibilities. I began to feel threatened. I tried to leave him, and he didn't take my rejection lightly. My best friend Monica helped me during these disastrous times in my life; she would come to support me whenever Alex had been drinking and was being disruptive. It was nice to have her with me. Alex disappointed me as I was with him to feel safe and protected. I lost all hopes of ever meeting any man who would genuinely love and protect me, a man whom I would feel safe with, ever. I thought that this would be the best that I could do; this was all that I had been destined for in my life.

Alex frequently caused damage to the property where we were living. He used to headbutt the walls putting holes in them. The following day, when he was sober, he would be repentant as he plastered and re-painted the walls, he always said how sorry he was and that he would never get drunk again. A typical pattern quickly emerged. He would feel guilty the day after one of his tirades and apologize for his behavior and actions. I was so tired of him doing this until it finally reached the point where I couldn't accept any more of his apologies. Sorry had become an empty word. When I told him I was leaving, he was outraged, and I realized that I needed to find a reason for not going back to him.

I thought maybe if I started seeing another man, then Alex would leave for good. I knew John from University, and we reunited again via social media, and so he became my next partner. John smoked marijuana and wasn't right for me at this point in my life; however, he was all I felt that I deserved. He was controlling and very manipulative.

My third suicide attempt of which I described earlier in this book, was with John. How was I to understand this being in the mental space that I was in? Going out with him was a way of getting rid of Alex, and my strategy worked. Alex got the message I had moved on without him. Unfortunately, around the same time as I left him, Alex's father had died, and his drinking became much worse. He lost his job. Then his apartment and his life ended up in the gutter.

Things also quickly went from bad to worse with my new boyfriend, John. I was working twelve-hour days, which left little time to dedicate to him, or our relationship. I guess that I didn't understand relationships or how to spend quality time with someone. I did not understand what being intimate with someone meant. Nor did I realize that relationships should be about giving and caring. I had nothing to offer emotionally. There wasn't any caring or understanding in me. All I wanted to do was to work. It's not surprising that things turned sour, and we argued a lot. He became abusive and punched a hole in my wall. I tried later to look on the bright side of this and thought that a hole in the wall was much better than a fist to my face!

It seemed as if I were trapped in a vicious cycle from which I couldn't escape. I would meet a man, fall into a relationship with him, but too quickly. Everyone else could see what was wrong. To me, it was just what I always did in a relationship. My friends shook their heads and warned me. I still felt like I needed him to keep me safe from predators, given how many men had hurt me until now. It turns out that the men whom I chose were the actual predators! John had made me afraid of being alone. I was also experiencing a sense of mistrust and fear that something terrible was about to happen to me. Being with him wasn't any better than my experiences with men, and I couldn't take anymore. We ended it. To get away from my problems, and to think about things, I went to Paris for the weekend. John still had the key to my apartment as his belongings were still there, so I hadn't asked for the key back. I later realized that this would be a mistake that I would live to regret.

I was having a great time until John turned on me for being away at the weekend and started sending me threats to ruin my life. As he still had the key to my apartment, his idea of a goodbye gift was to cause lots of damage to my lovely three-bedroom apartment. He wrote on my walls, using my lipstick. He opened some tins and scattered the fish inside them all over my clothes and in the drawers. He also destroyed my furniture. The damage he caused was astronomical and terrifying. Things got even crazier when he threatened to blow up my car if I went to the police.

I was frightened, depressed, and angry. I knew that I needed to get away from my apartment in Manchester as quickly as possible. Instead, my fear kicked in, and I went back to John because I didn't know what else to do. I feared what he might be capable of doing to me if I didn't go back to him.

Life was not good. I moved into another apartment with him and called it a fresh start. All was forgiven, but I still couldn't forget what he had put me through. John had always commented that I would never settle down being the free spirit that I am. I felt that I was sacrificing my freedom and my life by going back to him. It was inevitable that our relationship would get worse, and it did. There were more arguments, violence, and threats. Finally, he moved out of our apartment. I ran away to Spain to get away from him and his abuse.

While I was away, the apartment was broken into, and all of my possessions stolen. John worked in a prisoner rehabilitation center, so he should have been caring and responsible. John had known that I was away this weekend and so I was convinced that he, or one of the ex-convicts, was responsible. Whoever it was, had climbed through one of the windows and left it open afterward—the same as the front door.

During the time I spent with these men, I often sought validity for my actions. I used social media and asked for advice from my circle of friends. I used to write posts on my social media about what had happened to me.

"Why do I keep dating losers?"

"Why do I attract these men?"

"My house was burgled this weekend."

"I feel so unsafe here."

The posts helped me while I was going through the pain. I just needed to be cared for and to be told that everything would be okay.

My friends cautioned me that these men were stealing away my energy, and they warned me I was powerless when I was with them. I knew that they were right. I felt once again that I needed help and an escape. I was desperate to leave the turmoil in my life behind. Travel had been my salvation in the past, and I thought it would save me again. I felt free when I traveled. I was in tune with whom I was and what I wanted to be. Traveling freestyle was my passion, and I guess it will always be.

My Indian Heritage Denial

Anu Verma

From living a suppressed childhood life of 'to be seen but not heard,' I was not able to express myself or to show my true feelings. I understand now that the abuse I suffered would have had a significant impact on my ability to open up. I realized that I did not want to admit to being an Indian, and I despised what my culture believed and held dear.

When I left home at the age of eighteen to study, I finally found a way to enjoy myself and to have fun. When I went backpacking at the age of twenty-two, I finally found out how much I loved traveling and exploring new places and learning about new cultures, and in particular, I found a love for Buddhism. I also realized how much I loved meeting new people worldwide and learning more about them and going on adventure trips together. I learned about the different values and belief systems other than what I had growing up. When I returned to the UK at the age of twenty-four to study my master's degree, I found out how much I loved learning. Again, I met many different nationalities worldwide and lived in student accommodation with many Chinese students. I learned how to cook with them. I then went off to Canada at the age of twenty-five to work in cardiac rehabilitation and to learn more about the Canadian culture, which bought me so much joy.

I moved back to Manchester at the age of twenty-six, so I did lead an independent life, which is why I had lost most of the Indian values that I grew up having. Thankfully, I was not in my identity crisis of bleached blonde hair, fake tan, and bright pink lipstick; I now had my natural dark hair color and eased off on the make-up.

I may have looked more Indian though it still didn't bother me what people thought of me. I was not concerned about having a big house or a great car. I had a humble approach to life as I had seen how the Cambodians and Laos people lived and how happy they were just 'being.' Marriage neither interested me nor did having children. The thought of being married and settled bored me. Stability bored me. I craved adventure, and I desired variety in my life. I craved people who had a depth of character, and I craved uniqueness. I hung around with people who were not ordinary people nor stuck in their community cultures. I was independent and only had myself to keep happy. I still had so much traveling to do that all I cared about was ensuring that my backpack was kept safe. My backpack was my only treasure, oh, as well as the flags which I had bought from every country which I had visited up until then.

I attended festivals and dance clubs from the age of eighteen, predominantly where British English partygoers attended. I disliked attending the Indian family weddings and parties, so I made excuses to avoid going to them, and the most straightforward explanation for me was that I was overseas. I had a reputation of always traveling, which I didn't mind if it meant that I could avoid seeing all my extended family and family friends. I was even rude if I attended family gatherings and would say, "I have better things I could do than attending this wedding."

There was a big reason for this dislike of my Indian Heritage. It was based upon what I had been exposed to growing up. Apart from Gary, the other men who took advantage of me were Indians. So, I had a stigma against them, unfortunately. I was still too inexperienced and young to understand the significance of judgment back then. I also had a lot of resentment against my family and friends for not helping me through the abuse and turning a blind eye against what was happening to me. Everybody's reaction was always to just 'bury what had happened under the carpet,' 'forgive and forget,' and that 'life must go on.' Yes, I understand that life must go on, though, then do you blame me for becoming so confused with my identity and for not understanding what love is and for not understanding how to respect my body? What was self-respect, anyway? I had so many lessons still left to learn, though little did I realize that my life would get much worse before it got better.

My Indian Proposal

The following year in 2010, I had turned thirty, and given my poor track record with men so far, my mum suggested that it might be time for her to find me a good man. I don't blame her for trying to help me, and I was grateful. By this point, I needed any help I could get!

When I had previously met with Asian men whom my mum had introduced me to, the feedback was that I was too 'Westernized.' I reflected on what wasn't fitting into the Indian men's matrimonial partner requirements. It was me not cooking Indian meals; I wasn't housewife material as I enjoyed traveling alone and going out with friends. I had created my own life away from cultural influence.

I was working my day job while tutoring in the evenings and weekends, which took up all of my time during the weekdays, weeknights, and weekends, so when could I ever fit a partner into my life? I was still looking to invest more in another property and was looking at starting a business. I was undoubtedly not Indian wife material. I was, however, determined to attempt to invest in my life partner once and for all. I would learn to compromise, and I would be open-minded to men of my culture. It was time to make a fresh start.

My Mum's sister in India knew a lady trying to find a nice woman for her son. He was an optometrist and owned his own business in India. I was happy to be introduced to him based on what I had heard. My family and I were due to go to India not long afterward. I also intended to use this opportunity to meet Arjun for the first time.

Arjun came to meet me and things seemed great. He was tall, educated, and well-off. I was asked about the assets I owned, whether my property was paid for, and if I had a mortgage. What the rental income was, my salary, and whether I was in any debt. I may as well have been speaking to my financial advisor. I was even asked for my Curriculum Vitae! The amount of information required for a proposal in India felt overwhelming. It was similar to attending a job interview, and I was puzzled by it. Where were the usual questions men asked about hobbies, and what I liked to do in my free time, my favorite music, and so on? I felt that this proposition was strictly business. Nevertheless, I decided to embrace Indian culture and simply go with the flow.

VICTIM 2 VICTOR

I stayed in contact with Arjun when I returned to the United Kingdom. We spoke and messaged each other. Things were going great until I received one of the most disturbing images I had ever seen. He sent me a picture of his genitals. Whether I gave him the wrong impression about myself because of my free nature, carefree attitude, he didn't take me seriously. I also think the distance between us affected him, and I still don't know why he sent me this awful image. All I knew was that this guy had the wrong impression and a complete lack of respect for me. Starting a relationship on these terms would fail. I was not a girl who was happy to accept photographs like that. He had crossed a line. I cut my ties to him, and I blocked him from my life.

I found this experience disturbing, especially after everything I had been through as a child and later on in my adult life. It made me curious too. So much so I looked into the mentality of men in India and why they regarded women as sexual objects. I don't mean to generalize or judge anyone, but Western women are unfortunately seen in a poor light. They are thought of as being forward, open, and easy—American movies generated mostly this view. I am still unsure why any man would think that by sending pictures of his private parts to a woman, he could win her heart! Do men feel that their size is so essential to a woman that this is all they need to please a woman? Is it women themselves who have fueled this thinking, in their desire for sexual satisfaction? I will leave it to you to decide.

Traveling Again

I then decided that it was time to leave my destructive life in Manchester once and for all. I moved all of my belongings to my family's home in Coventry and packed my backpack to go on a long adventure again. I went to India, Nepal, Burma, Thailand, Indonesia, and the Philippines. My travels took me on thirty-six flights in three months. I was in flight mode, and my main objective for this trip was to keep on running away as far away as I could, and as fast as I could. My adventure turned out to be a huge learning curve, and not quite what I had expected. It was going to cause me more grief, stress, and trauma.

India

My family was reluctant to let me travel alone to India. They begged me not to go.

"Anu, please don't go to India alone," my mother pleaded. "It's far too dangerous for a young girl to be on her own. In India, single women are not thought of as people. They are regarded as things."

There was political turmoil in India, and most of it aimed at women. I pleaded with them and made a fuss until they consented to allow me to travel alone. I was naïve and lost. I soon found out why they were so concerned for my safety.

I did enjoy some of my experiences in India. I traveled from Punjab to Delhi, then on to Nepal in the Himalayas. While I was there, I wandered through the Pashupatinath Temple, which is one of the four most religious sites in Asia for devotees of Shiva, so I spent some time in meditation here. I toured the Boudha Stupa, which comprises the five most promising elements representing Buddha (earth, air, water, fire, and space) in the Stupas architecture. I found so much peace and tranquility here. The thirty-six-meter-high stupa of Buddha is the center of Tibetan Buddhism in Nepal with many monasteries around it. They played this beautiful Tibetan musical mantra called 'Om Mani Padme Hum,' and I listen to this even now as it takes me back to Nepal and the feelings I had out there of freedom, happiness, and peace. Feelings that I had always struggled to obtain back in the UK. I trekked the Chitwan National Park, which is the first national park in Nepal. I took a helicopter ride over Mount Everest, the highest mountain globally, measuring 8,848m (29,029 feet) in height. I have always dreamed of seeing Mount Everest even as a child as it has always fascinated me, and here I was, living my dream. Life felt amazing.

Victim 2 Victor

Nepal was known for its hospitality and was one of the best places in the world for a single woman to visit traveling on her own. Hundreds of travelers visited Nepal every year to test their climbing skills in the Himalayas and go on trekking tours. Traveling through it and breathing the clear air of the Himalayas was terrific, but little did I know then that going back into India would take a menacing turn.

I went on a bus from Punjab to Delhi, and I was so tired that I fell asleep. When I woke up, a businessman was sitting very close to me and touching me sexually. I had enough courage to tell him to get lost. I raised my voice so that everyone on the bus could hear what I said. The other passengers looked shocked, and the businessman stared at me with hatred in his eyes. I left the bus and quickly got on the next one going to the international area from the domestic section of the airport. I was terrified as I sat on the bus. I was alone and unprotected. My experiences so far had shown me that my family was right, even though my travel planner told me that India was a popular place for women like me to travel alone. Despite all the other warnings and dire media reports, I decided that the best way to deal with the situation would be to surrender to what was happening and go with the flow. This was not, however, the best piece of advice that I could have given to myself.

I was only one of two people on the bus. The other passenger was a man who kept looking at me and talking to the driver. They were laughing at stupid jokes, pointing and gesturing at me. I had a horrible feeling about that and was afraid for my safety. I didn't know what these men would do to me, but they could easily molest and abuse me. Imagine my relief when the bus stopped. I got off immediately. As I waited for another bus to take me to my hotel, I read about a gang rape incident in Delhi. I began to wonder then why I hadn't listened to my family's concerns when I told them that I was going to India alone.

According to data at that time, a rape took place every fifteen minutes in India, making ninety-six rape incidents every day. That's around thirty-five thousand cases a year. Reports of brutal rape, and violence against women, had given India a reputation for being one of the worst places in the world to be female. A female traveling alone was an advertisement for sexual abuse. I also read about a twenty-three-year-old student beaten and gang-raped on a moving bus in New Delhi. She died later of severe injuries to her abdomen, intestines, and genitals due to the brutality of the assault. Five men and a juvenile were arrested. Four of the men had been sentenced. The other convicted man hung himself during the trial, but the minor was freed. He was still roaming the streets.

My exploits in Delhi were nothing compared to what happened to me in Kerala, on the southwestern Malabar Coast of India. As I was heading back to my hotel, some local men, naked from the waist down, started to chase me. I found out later that the disintegration of the Nayar Army had led to a lot of men wandering around the area. They were naked from the waist down, as a sign of rebellion. They wanted freedom. Why they thought that this behavior made them free, I will never know. It was horrifying. I ran to the nearest hotel screaming that I was being chased, and I begged for help.

A seemingly nice chap came to my rescue. He offered to drive me back to my hotel. I got onto the moped behind him because I was afraid of the others. I was thanking God, too, for a rescuer. As we traveled down the road, I didn't understand why he started to nudge me. He told me to put my hands around him for safety reasons. I suddenly became aware of the situation I was in, and I began to distrust him. I refused, as emphatically as I could. When we arrived at my hotel, he blatantly asked if he could come to my room for sex. I shook my head and ran into the hotel.

I couldn't help thinking, why me? I couldn't enjoy my trip to India because of these predatory men. Everywhere I went, I felt as if a man wanted to touch, rape, or hurt me in some way. Not long ago, I let a man get away with rape because I wasn't strong enough. Here I was in India, defending myself and standing up for myself. I felt inner strength, and I felt resilience; maybe I needed this trip to start my healing journey from all the trauma that I had experienced.

VICTIM 2 VICTOR

Up until recently, crimes against women continued in India unabated. Nothing happened, and the perpetrators walked away without punishment. Home office statistics at the time of writing this book suggested that alleged perpetrators in more than ninety-eight percent of rape cases reported to the police, are allowed to go free. Only one-point seven percent of rapes result in a charge or summons being issued. Is it any wonder that so few women report these incidents to the authorities? They are suffering from the trauma of being raped, and the consequences of hoping that the situation will simply go away.

Newspapers reported that there was almost total impunity for sexual assault or rape. Once upon a time, ordinary passersby would intervene and help the victim until roving gangs had knives and guns. While I was in India, a man was killed by a youth gang as he tried to protect his young niece from harassment. Many cities in India were listed as unsafe for solo travel, especially for females. It has saddened me to see a beautiful country tainted by its sexually hungry men.

Unfortunately, the predators weren't finished with me. I was on my way back to Delhi when a seventy-year-old grandpa sat next to me on the bus and had the most sordid look in his eyes as he stared at me, the look of someone about to harm. He started to move his hands toward me. Since I was sitting on the inside seat, next to the window, there was little that I could do. I was trapped, so I screamed. Fortunately, a lovely couple was sitting behind me. They abruptly asked the older man to move so that the wife could sit next to me instead. I thanked God for them that day.

Indonesia

A part of my travels that I don't want to forget was in Indonesia. The country was home to one hundred and fifty volcanoes. I traveled to Bali, and I found Ubud, a profoundly spiritual place that resonated with me. Ubud was a center for traditional crafts and dance with one of the most famous landscapes in Southeastern Asia. Ancient holy shrines included Goa Gajah or the Elephant Cave, and Gunung Kawi with shrines cut out of the rock. Yoga and meditation retreats were easy to find. I began to practice and immerse myself in the healing energies and power of yoga. It was my first-time practicing yoga, and it is there that my love for yoga and meditation came alive. I met a lovely family who invited me to their home. They gave me a Ganesha to take with me on my travels. It would help to protect me and to bring me luck. Ganesha, the elephantine head, was a symbol of strength and power. It would safeguard me from life's physical and mental challenges, and that was just what I needed on my travels!

I had a late-night flight between Lombok and Flores and hadn't booked anywhere to stay that night, so once I arrived at the airport, I made some calls using my lonely planet guide, and after a couple of calls with all the hotels being booked, there was one room available. I took the taxi there and went to check-in. There was a security guard who escorted me to my room for the night. It was the last room vacant, and so I was delighted to have a place to crash for the night. I was tired, and so I quickly got dressed and into bed. It was the tropical season, so I ensured that I had a fly spray to keep the mosquitos at bay.

It didn't take me long to fall into a deep sleep and I was suddenly awoken by the disturbing sounds of wasps buzzing away above me to the right where the light was. There must have been thirty of them, and they were so loud that I panicked though I was grateful to have the fly spray right by my bedside. I grabbed the bottle and sprayed all above me and where the wasps were. I sprayed and sprayed nearly all the container as I heard the wasps falling on the floor one by one; they were that heavy that I could hear them thudding loudly. This was a victory! Once the last of the wasps died, I jumped out of bed and ran near the door because I was shaken. I turned the light on and saw all the wasps on the floor; there were so many of them. Tired and exhausted, I fell back to sleep.

The next morning, as I got ready amidst all the wasps on the floor, I felt like a convict though my safety was my main concern. I went downstairs to reception to check out, and the lady looked at my key and had a very concerned look on her face. She turned to her manager, who was also in shock as she stared at me. The receptionist asked if I was okay?

I replied, "Yes, why wouldn't I be?"

She explained in her broken English that the security guard should have never given me that room as it was infested and dangerous with a wasp nest.

I already knew this because I had murdered twenty of them, and they were on the floor waiting to be swept up and buried somewhere. I explained that I was okay and that I needed the sleep. She didn't want any money and told me that the room was 'on the house.' She felt guilty as did her manager though I felt relieved that I was able to rest and to plan on where to go next. I look back to this day and thank whoever is looking down on me that I could walk away from that infested room unharmed, and this experience taught me a precious lesson to never take anything for granted.

After my one month visit to Indonesia, I felt that I was finally attracting some good into my life. I was blessed to have been able to travel there and to meet such spiritual and loving souls on my journey. I cannot wait to go back to Ubud, see the beauty of nature again, and the friendly people who were so kind to me.

Burma

Burma was my next destination, and I loved it. I visited Buddhist temples and retreats, where I was able to find inner peace. I enjoyed the Buddhist culture, and as in my previous trips to South East Asia, I felt calm and accepted. I played at being a tourist. I traveled to the Schwedagon Pagoda, Inle Lake, Ananda Temple, and Mandalay Hill. I joined groups of tourists at the Yangon Zoological Garden, Lampi Island, and Marine National Park. Burma is now known as 'Myanmar' and is unlike any other country in Southeast Asia. Except that all of them are the friendliest countries in the world. People smile and go out of their way to help foreigners, often inviting them into their homes for a cup of tea. These people love their country and want to share it with others.

Burma is also a Buddhist country. When I went there, religion played a vital role in daily life. Monks in red robes, and Buddhist nuns in pink robes, walked on the streets and shopped in the market. It was peaceful and spiritual inside the temples, which seemed to be everywhere, and I relished this peace. As I traveled, I found that I didn't want to get too close to anyone I met. I kept my travel buddies at arm's length and only spent as much time with them as I needed to. Why was this? I guess I was a travel commitment-phobe and not wanting to feel obliged to stay in a place for too long as I desired to leave so that I could carry on exploring at a fast pace. I had so much I needed to see and so much that I needed to do that I was always worried that by getting too close to travel buddies, it might slow me down, or I would get distracted and not want to continue on my own. I guess you could say that I was easily influenced, and so lacked inner strength. I was still vulnerable and still had so much development ahead of me, and these travels were just the start of this journey.

Philippines

It was during this part of the trip that I noticed my spirituality and self-development journey developing. I realized that I was worth so much more than what was happening to me. I was not a sex toy. I was educated. I was talented. I had a lot to offer. I would survive, and the light within me began to shine brighter.

I met a fellow traveler in Boracay in the Philippines. He wanted to become friends with me. We had a great time on a sailing yacht cruise, and I left the following day. That's how I traveled in the past, in a very free-spirited way and without making plans in advance. I left the island without saying goodbye to him. Why did I owe him any explanation? To my chagrin, I received a nasty message via social media. He was upset that I had left without telling him. He wrote something insulting about being used. I deleted the message, and him, from my social media. He acted as if I had slept with him, which I had not. I don't know what the problem was, but the last thing I had on my mind during my travels was being intimate with anybody. This was another real milestone for my personal growth.

I continued traveling through the Philippines, where I found a silent retreat in a small village. Bahay Kalipay's raw food and the yoga retreat house is a self-sustainable community and sees the vision of living in harmony with each other and the community. There was no toilet paper, no processed food or drink, and I completed a vegan detox program, eating only raw food. I did a coconut juice fast also to cleanse out my system. It was challenging, and I had detox headaches, which were a nuisance, but it was peaceful. The village itself was beautiful and calm. It gave me the happiness and peace that I needed.

This was the perfect place for me during this time of my life. I was away from the societal pressures of the rat race, which we get sucked into in the Western world to achieve and accomplish continually in a fast-paced culture. This retreat helped me to slow down and to appreciate just 'being.'

I was very apprehensive about leaving the Philippines and returning to the United Kingdom, but it was time to go home. I wondered what I would find when I arrived home. How would it feel? I will always remember my journey through the countries of South East Asia, where I learned the healing power of Buddhism and felt the friendliness of the people. I saw so many beautiful temples and landscapes. I hope that I will be able to go back there one day.

Returning to the UK

When I returned to the United Kingdom after my three-month life-changing trip where I felt as free as a bird, I attracted even more problems from damaged men. They took away my power yet again. Why I let them into my life, I will never know. Perhaps I was a magnet for needy men who carried a lot of baggage. Maybe my energy was saying that I was needy too, and wanted a man in my life. But by then, I felt like I deserved much more in terms of love and quality in a man. I had started to trust in the future, and that eventually, a man would think of me in favorable terms. All I needed to do was to find him.

Before long being back in the UK, I fell into a relationship with Matt, who was a very dangerous, controlling, and manipulating man with whom I would learn another precious lesson. It was an unhealthy relationship from the start. Later on, I learned about narcissism and realized that he portrayed all the traits of this personality disorder. He used to make me feel awful if I didn't drive over to his place and see him at least twice a week. He used to call me fat and had me on a 'Special K' diet with him where we ate 'Special K' cereal twice a day and then the main meal. He would play mind games with me for control, telling me that my friends and family weren't on my side.

I found myself becoming distant from anybody who had ever been close to me. If I made new friends, Matt would research them on social media and make up a story about who they were. He would pretend that their partners were dubious, and that I was being manipulated into their gang. He tried to convince me that I shouldn't contact my friends and family as they didn't care for me. I was shocked by some stuff he came out with, but I still somehow believed him.

Matt lived in a small house with a CCTV security system installed. He was living in fear and paranoia as he had so many people who disliked him. He was on bad terms with his former friends and family. It always seemed to be a problem with money. Matt had inherited a lot from his father but lost it because of some dodgy dealings. Finding out about him losing so much money should have been a red flag to me, but I wanted so much to believe in him. His inherited property had bank loans on it. He had borrowed money from the banks using the property as security and refused afterward to pay it back.

VICTIM 2 VICTOR

Matt also had a very frail mum whom he was supposed to care for and help. I found out later that he was abusing her financially and mentally. She was terrified of him and had learned to hide her cash. Everyone else and his mum knew that Matt would take whatever they had. Matt was a bad man all the way through, but I couldn't see it. I had my rose-tinted glasses on. I was being manipulated horrendously into thinking that he was good. I was also still not entirely sure who I was. Maybe again, like how I felt in my previous relationships, I thought he was the only type of man I deserved.

There were signs which I feel were sent to me from a higher place. My angels, spirits, or whoever it was that was looking out for me and protecting me. If I took some photos of us on my phone, a strange black blob would show up over him. It even appeared when he sat next to his mum in a photo I had taken during Christmas. I had never seen this back blob occur on any of my photos before, so this was a new and exciting occurrence. At the time, Matt explained to me that I had a demon who was attached to me; hence, why it was being expressed over his face. Again, his manipulation was at work. I always knew that it wasn't me who had the demon; it was him, though, at the time, I chose to ignore it and to turn a blind eye to this important sign. I would later find out that whatever he was doing to me, his mum was being treated far worse. The black blob was an accurate indication that this man was dangerous.

The turning point in our relationship came when he took me to a Rolex event, featuring Watches of Switzerland. Matt flaunted the watch he had bought, using my credit card. I was heavily manipulated into believing he had lots of money in his bank and didn't have a credit card with him. He promised that the money would be wired straight to my bank account. As you can probably guess, no money was transferred!

He acted as if he was a millionaire. As we sat around a table with the others at the show, I mentioned that he hadn't bought the watch. I didn't realize the consequences of what I had said until we left the event. Matt shouted at me, asking me how I dared embarrass him like that. He was crying, and the trip home from the convention turned out to be the worst I had ever experienced. I felt like the lowest human on the planet. I was crying too and trying to defend myself. I told Matt that it was the truth. He hadn't bought the watch. I also let him know that he still owed me eight thousand dollars for it. Until he paid that back, it was not his watch to flaunt. I had gone through too much up until this point just to let 'another' man get away with taking advantage of me. I was not going to allow this to happen. I knew there was a shift in my self-worth by this point as I felt strong, and I felt resilient.

Matt's dark side came out when we arrived home. He pointed his finger at my face as he started to become even angrier. He threatened me that it would be the last time that I embarrassed him. I was feeling very uncomfortable by then. I asked him to move out of my way so that I could leave. He told me to use the back door. I was suspicious of this as he had buried his dog in his back garden. I began to worry about what he might be capable of doing to me if I did leave by the back door and had to climb over his fence.

I pushed him aside to run out of the front door as soon as I could. I jumped into my car and sped away. Matt chased me in his car as I was trying to get away from him. Unfortunately, I had to stop when I was approaching the motorway. Part of me deep inside was still hoping that he would catch me and make amends. Until I remembered that he still owed me the money for the watch, and his temper was awful! I understand now that I was naïve in giving Matt my credit card to buy the watch. Why did I lend him my credit card? I am unsure what came over me, which led me to make this costly mistake. However, all I can say is that I was under some heavy influence of manipulation and control, for those who of you who are reading this and who have been in similar situations, you would understand. I was vulnerable and weak and suffering from low self-esteem, and so it would have been easy for anybody at this point to take full advantage of me. Of course, he didn't keep his promise to pay me back. I ended the relationship while still begging him to return my money.

Victim 2 Victor

My intuition gave me the strength to say, 'NO MORE,' and I felt so relieved that I did not have to experience any further hurt from this man. The only thing left to do was to try to get my money back. This was okay for me to handle because money was nothing in the grand scheme of things. It was better for him to have my money than my dignity or my life.

Even after the relationship had ended, I had many sleepless nights feeling stressed, anxious, and with my hair starting to thin. Before I began to look into how I might retrieve my money, I filed a small claim against him at court. He didn't reply, so I won the case. I now have a County Court judgment against him for monetary sums. He did eventually take me to court, trying to appeal the rulings against him. Thank heavens, the Judge didn't believe him, and I won the court case again. He even tried to appeal that Judge's decision and lost the application also.

To this day, Matt is still paying me back what he owes me, as ordered by the Court. Rolex has some of the most expensive watches you can buy. The prices range from five thousand pounds to four hundred thousand, or more. The watches are a status symbol, and that was what Matt was all about, status and looking like he had money.

My first ever feeling of recognition as someone with worth, came when I won in court. I had regained my power after it had been lost in yet another harmful relationship. I hadn't ever experienced this feeling before, and I wanted to feel this way so much more.

Anu Verma

Chapter VIII: A New Relationship and a Broken Dream

When my relationship with Matt ended, I lost lots of weight, and my hair was falling out from the stress of everything that I had been through. I wasn't taking care of myself or practicing yoga like I should have been, as this would have helped me during the stressful court case. I needed to recuperate.

I traveled to Peru to seek some adventure and to get away from the hurt and the surroundings, again, trying to find some peace. I was still hurting and vulnerable and no way ready to be in another relationship though unfortunately, when you are in such a state, you seek security and comfort. If only I felt secure, strong, and confident enough to spend some time alone so that I could heal and recover from all the hurt that I had experienced so far.

I was in a vicious circle of self-destruction. I hadn't learned enough from my past relationships, so this time, I ended up attracting a serial cheater and a man who again possessed many narcissistic traits, borderline sociopath.

Ben was a German dental implantologist with a very prestigious practice in Frankfurt. He was a specialist in implants, using CEREC technology, a new state-of-the-art method of reconstruction tooth restorations, and he owned a clinic in Berlin. He was living with his mum. As the caring son, he had hired a cleaner who helped around the house and ironed his shirts. He also had a cook who provided their meals. They were a very noble family, but Ben had a problem. He drank a lot of vodkas every day.

He was a salsa dancer too, and I love Latin American music. With his skillful dancing and charm, he soon had me wrapped around his little finger. I thought Ben was a captivating and positive man. We had a great time in Peru, enjoying visiting the spiritual site of Machu Picchu and other wonderful and historic cities such as Arequipa, Cusco, and Puno. Our personalities seemed to click.

I believed that he was about to propose to me, and I would move to Berlin with him. How trusting I was! When I went back home to the UK, and he went back home to Berlin, we continued a long-distance relationship for a few months. I would travel over to him every other weekend, or he would travel over to me. We continued exploring different parts of the UK while he was here, and we explored various sites of Europe. A few months had passed, I was planning on moving in with him in his home and with his mum. I was also in the process of having some business cards made for the medical tourism business we were going to set up together. I was going to help him by promoting his dental services in the United Kingdom. His contact in Berlin made the business cards for us.

One weekend when I visited Ben, he left me with his mum and went to a conference. As he was away, I could not get hold of him. He told me that he didn't have any phone reception in his room and that he couldn't contact me as much as usual. When he did call, he said that the days were long, and he hadn't enjoyed the presentations. Ben was very good at hiding the truth while emphasizing certain aspects of the event leading me to ask questions.

I had just left his home that weekend and traveled back to the UK, and the next day I received an email from a woman named Anna who explained to me that Ben was seeing five other women besides us. I couldn't believe it. I didn't know what to make of the situation. At first, I thought she was envious.

I confronted Ben about this email, and he denied everything and was angry that I was even speaking with him about this. He made me believe that Anna wanted to destroy my relationship with him and that I should ignore her. Anna then put me in touch with another woman who Ben had deceived. Victoria was based in Panama, and I emailed her to ask if what Anna was saying was true. She replied that she did not want anything to do with the vile man.

I decided to investigate further via social media, and by asking all of his staff members who were no longer with him, we were able to locate the other women. So, we started talking, emailing, and exchanging each of our stories. After that, everything began to make sense. Anna was Ben's long-term girlfriend whom he had been with for five years, and she had seen him with all of these other women from all over the world though, for some reason, she still stayed with him. It was a mutual contact between Ben and Anna, who was arranging the business cards for me, which is how my email information got passed over to Anna.

I found out afterward that he was meeting one of his girlfriends at the conference when he left me at home with his mum. I realized that his mum and sister must have known what he was doing. Were they laughing at me behind my back? He would video call us when he was away from the girl whom he was with at the time. I remember one occasion when he was video calling me from his car. He had one of his other girls inside his cousins' house. His cousin came out to help Ben with his bags and said hello to me on the video call. I am still curious about how he managed to introduce all of us to his family and friends.

Another time I was at his friend's house, and they spoke in German. I didn't understand what they were saying, which I am sure was convenient for Ben. He left the room to use his phone. Then he came back telling me that the caller was a patient who had issues with the treatment he or she was receiving. That was a lie! I found out later that he had been speaking to one of his other girls. On another occasion, Ben left me with his mum and went out of the room to talk on the phone. It sounded as if a woman was shouting at him. I later found out that the phone call was from one of his other women who weren't happy with his behavior. He told me again that a patient had called him as she was unhappy with another doctor, and that he was asked to sort out the issue—so many lies. I am not sure how he managed to keep up with them. He must have been exhausted.

He would visit his local girlfriend for food and whatever else he wanted if it were a weekday. He returned home afterward, to sit in the bath while video calling the other girls and me. He would meet his other women while he was away from home or invite them to stay over at his house.

Before I found out about his cheating, I left a couple of suitcases at his home. I thought that we were so much in love. He was even designing a wardrobe for me. Perhaps he thought that I would be so impressed with his efforts that I would be sucked into his life, despite the deceit and lies. Really? Would a wardrobe be enough to make me turn my whole life in the United Kingdom upside down, give up my career, my family, and the life that I had, to be with him in his sick world? It might have worked, had I not known the truth about his other girlfriends. I found out later that he had also asked Maria, his Indonesian girlfriend, to move in with him during September, while I was planning on moving in with him in March. I am still not sure what plan he had for both of us in his home.

My relationship with him ended after some messaging back and forth. I finally asked him to send all of my stuff back, which was still at his house. He obligingly shipped all of it to me.

I thought that this could be why he needed to drink so much -- his way of diluting the lies and cheating. He couldn't live with the deceit and have a healthy, happy life. I wondered if he ever had a good night's sleep, or if he turned to drink to escape reality. Ben's reality? Not being true to himself or the surrounding people, he must have had mental health issues. When I think back now, it was pretty scary how he played me. It was a dangerous game.

When I was introduced to Maria in Indonesia, we created a WhatsApp group. Here we exchanged dates and photos. We were disgusted with him and plotted our revenge. We decided to tell the world what he had done, using social media. When our posts went live, and Ben got hold of them, he tried to sue us. There were laws against defamation of character in the United Kingdom, being dealt with under European law. I was the easiest target to sue. The other women in Indonesia and South America were more difficult to pursue through legal proceedings because of the different laws. He didn't get very far with them. After the police had questioned me, they decided that it was a personal issue. They didn't have any jurisdiction over what we had said on social media.

So here I was, a 35-year-old British- Asian female, who had already had a string of failed relationships and bad experiences up until date. I lacked hope that I would ever meet a nice man who would care for me or who I could start a family.

Being with these men had taken away my internal power, strength, and beliefs about myself; I trusted too quickly. I am aware of this. I mentioned earlier about how I have always believed that I am protected from high above, whether it be a higher spirit, my angel… it could even be my intuition, which still has a way of ensuring my safety and protection. Whatever it is, I feel that Anna was sent down to save me from this evil man. Receiving her emails and knowing that I did not have to remain in such a toxic relationship reassured me that I needed to regain trust in myself and believe that I was worthy of real love. I did not deserve to be with such deceitful and dishonest men. It was from this experience that I felt inner strength, more self-worth, and self-belief. I believed in myself and that I was capable of fighting for what I deserved. Men could not easily take advantage of me anymore, and so I decided to make a change in my life and my choice of men.

Chapter IX: Marriage

It had been a few months of feeling sad and trying to heal myself. I took up yoga again and started studying for my certification in teaching yoga. I was also very much into healing energies by this point and had become a Tera-Mai Seichem Reiki Master, Emotional Freedom Therapist, and a Hypnotherapist. The training for my qualifications assisted me in my healing, and I was on my way to a more positive future. I met some very spiritual and positive people along my journey who were helping me in my growth and transformation.

Marie, my therapist, helped me through the darkest times, and she took me to Arthur Findlay College, where we studied mediumship for a week, which was a life-changer for me. I started to believe in spirits and that there is a higher self beyond this physical form, which are our bodies. Finally, I thought things are looking up. I felt like I was in a better place.

I then took a girls' holiday to get over my latest crisis and traveled to Spain with friends. That's where I met Paul. We had a common interest, which was that our ex-partners had recently cheated on both of us, and so our heartache brought us together. I was not ready for another relationship as I felt exhausted from the ongoing failed relationships. I was now on a route to success with my healing knowledge and gaining my therapy certifications. However, Paul was genuine, kind, down to earth, honest. He was everything that all of my ex-boyfriends were not.

I can see now that the numerous men who came into my life were all part of my personal development. They may well have been sent to me to teach me a valuable lesson, but that concept took me some time to get right. The answer was there all along; it isn't wise to fall into a relationship with just anyone. I desired to be loved, and I needed acceptance. I wanted to be cared for, I felt insecure, so I trusted all of them too quickly at the beginning of the relationship, as I was about to do again when I met Paul.

When we traveled home to the United Kingdom, we lived one hundred and fifty miles apart, but we still called each other and spoke numerous times daily. We went on holiday and enjoyed the weekends together. We partied, and I still felt insecure. I frequently checked his social media pages to see which posts he was 'liking,' who he was following, and how he acted with females. I often accused him of flirting. I had been so damaged by the previous relationships that I couldn't trust him. I often cried all night. It was a regular occurrence for Paul and me to break up. I couldn't believe that he wasn't sleeping with other women. There was no evidence of him ever cheating on me, so I understand that my insecurity feelings were more reflective of my struggles with men. The feelings I had for him remained in conflict with each other.

We had been together for two years, I then fell pregnant, and we decided it was time to 'tie the knot.' So, when I was three months pregnant, we got married. I wasn't able to commit fully to it. I had too many doubts, although I tried my best to keep an open mind. I remember thinking that my feelings could change; my love for Paul would grow stronger and more profound, especially when our son arrived. Paul was his father! At the same time, I was growing and changing a lot because of my yoga and meditation practices.

VICTIM 2 VICTOR

During my relationship with Paul, I wanted to become a healer and had become a qualified yoga teacher, hypnotherapist, an emotional freedom therapist, and a Reiki Master. The seeds for this had been planted. I was already doing well in my training as a strategic intervention coach. This led eventually to me attending Tony Robbins' seminars, detox retreats, and I felt that I was finally on my way to being healed. I started to invest as much money as I could into my journey of self-discovery, and I desperately wanted Paul to come with me. He was drawn to the idea of changing and to become a more spiritual person, but that was all. He wasn't doing anything about it, and the inevitable happened; we grew worlds apart because of the way I was changing.

After Noah was born, I had counseling sessions. I wasn't in a great place and feeling the way I did about Paul made things even more complicated. My counselor and I discussed *Maslow's Hierarchy of Needs* and at what stages we were both during this time of our life.
Our basic needs weren't the same, and the goals were a million miles apart. Yet Paul had created a safe place for me during our four-year relationship, where I could take advantage of these therapies, to grow and develop. I will always thank him from the bottom of my heart for this unique, life-changing gift.

Despite how much I loved my son, I didn't find the first few months as a mother an easy time because I was suffering from postpartum depression. This usually includes intense feelings of helplessness, insomnia, irritability, and boredom. I suffered from all of these symptoms. If they remain untreated, postpartum depression can last for months or even longer. I realized through my counseling that childbirth also triggered psychological issues around abuse. Antidepressants, counseling, or hormone therapy are often prescribed. I just wanted to feel like the real me again. I had quit my job so that I could take care of Noah. Having such a strong work ethic that I have had my whole life, I never realized that this would have made the depression worse, as I had lost my independence.

I was so happy when a boss at my previous company contacted me. He wanted me back at work in the organization. So, after eight months' absence, I had a job again and felt as if my independence had returned. Noah was safe and happy too. My relationship with my parents became stronger since the birth of Noah, and they helped me with his upbringing. Having moved away from home at eighteen, I had lost touch with my family and my friends, whom I grew up with. I felt resentment toward my family and friends for not helping me through my journey though I realized that whatever happened to me was not their fault. They did not have the mental capacity to deal with my issues. It was my journey to take and my journey to learn from. Reuniting with everybody in my home town again was a blessing. With time, Paul and I started to get along better also, despite our differences.

Noah

Noah had a Buddhist blessing at the Nagarjuna Kadampa Meditation Center when he was born. The ceremony was attended by all of mine and Paul's close family and friends. Noah looked very smart in his shirt and trousers. It was a very peaceful afternoon and was enjoyed by everybody. This was a ceremony to bring peace into our worlds. It was non-traditional, and there was no dress code. The ceremony consisted of a 'Tara Puja.' 'Tara' is the meditation deity and "mother of liberation" and represents the virtues of success in work and achievements. A 'Puja' is the name for ceremonies that involve offerings or gifts. We prayed and meditated, and the ceremony was filled with beautiful energy.

I wanted Noah to grow up feeling at peace with himself and others. It was my dream for him to feel secure and loved. I would never want him to go through what I did. From my own experiences, I now feel more aware and more alert, which will set him up for better than I had. I will keep him safe. I believe that his Buddhist blessing has given him the energy to connect with others with compassion. This will allow him to understand himself as he grows. He will discover an awakening and have a mind that is full of awe and humility. Buddhism is not only about being human but the best human we can be. It connects us to the Earth and the belief that there is more to life than what is on the surface. Ultimately, through realization and experience, it's not about institutions or divine authority, or for those who think of themselves as religious.

I do want Noah to experience life to its full extent and to go through situations that will make him healthy and wise. I know that he will have obstacles to overcome. Without problems or taking risks, he will never learn or be able to grow as a person. I am looking forward to taking him to the spiritual places I visited, such as Nepal, India, Bali, and Burma. Those unique places opened my eyes to having a beautiful life, and without the need for material possessions, a life based on love and peace. I have learned that we can make a simple life happy and successful. I want Noah to be rich in this way. The western world is often based on technology, competition amongst peers, and confusion. I want Noah to discover that there is more to his life than this "modern living." Through the influence of societal pressures, I was raised to believe that all we needed was a nice big house and a nice car. During my self-development journey, I realized that having a large home or a car would not make me happy. I needed more in my life, I needed connection, I needed love, and I needed adventure.

I started to see that I was different from the societal norms and status I had been raised. I had broken free of this mindset and went out to seek what truly brought me joy. I discovered the joys of travel and how being genuine and authentic to ourselves and learning about various cultures brought me joy.

Staying in the shamanic villages up in the mountains in Laos and the Philippines, the locals had no electricity, yet they were filled with so much happiness. Life is about how much love you have inside of you to give. Life is about contribution, and a common question which I ask myself regularly is, "How can I add value to others?"

We get sucked into just acceptance and greed; I know I sure was. I always wanted more until I learned to let this greed go. It has taken me many years to come to this state of realization, so it hasn't just happened overnight. Whether you are reading this book or starting on your healing journey, you have already reached a point of self-realization.

And Me Today

Today, I feel blessed and grateful for the life which I have led. I have no regrets, and I thank every soul whoever entered into my life. Every person within this book has taught me a valuable lesson, and they have contributed toward my growth, and I can only be grateful for this.

To enhance my growth and mindset, I make time for meditation and yoga. These rituals keep me focused, free of stress, and free of worries. I also sometimes go away with friends, if the time is right, because I have learned that life is about balance, and like everyone else, I need this. In contrast, I am so happy and blessed to have Noah, my boy. He is the best thing in my life. I still have therapy sessions and attend seminars to continue with my personal development. I hope to hop on an airplane soon to see some of my favorite places. I would love to revisit the Galapagos Islands for its magnificent nature, Palawan in the Philippines, for its exotic beaches and white sand, and Ubud again, in Bali, for its spirituality and tranquility. I will never forget the magical time that I spent there.

My boy and I have already gone to so many places within the UK together. I want my son to be proud of his heritage. We went to the Natural History Museum in London on one occasion, and he could explore this as a scientist would. He loved touching and playing with the educational tools and learning how they worked. We have also been to the Buddhist Exhibition at the British Library, where we met my dear friend, Lisa, who lives in London. I am learning to make the most out of my life, spend time with my son, and, most importantly, I now have the freedom to be the creator of my own life.

VICTIM 2 VICTOR

Sharing My Story

I have been sharing my story since my healing journey began in 2012. I have attended workshops and spiritual groups where we share our stories, and we talk about our devastating situations with previous partners, which have involved different types of abuse.

The next part of this book goes into more detail, describing my healing journey to victory. I discuss techniques such as reiki, emotional freedom therapy, meditation, yoga, and my spiritual life coaching, which gave me the ability to reclaim my life. I provide scientific explanations about abuse and trauma and the psychological effects this can have on us and how it is possible to heal.

Becoming a mother gave me the drive and motivation to start my writing career, so I feel that I have Noah to thank the most as he has given me the inspiration to fulfill my dreams and aspirations. My mission is to add value wherever I can and leave my legacy behind, one of which my son would be proud of someday.

A heartwarming experience I recently had was during my charity work. I was at the shelter where I helped the homeless and spoke with a lady who had lost everything. She had reached the point where she was simply surviving each day as it came. I couldn't help but look at my life and see why her life was so different. I then analyzed that the main differences between her and me seemed to be willpower and determination. These are the tools required to help one to succeed if they wish to change their life for the better. Will and determination were the main attributes that saw me through my earlier struggles and trauma.

Sharing our stories made me realize how grateful I am to have had the strength to plow through all the hurt and the pain that I have experienced. Where did this strength come from within me? I will never know, although I believe that having grace and faith have helped me throughout my journey. I was born a Hindu. I continue to respect its many Gods, but I don't practice any form of organized religion. I have instead taken parts of those which resonate deeply within me. I believe that God is within all of us; however, we conceive God to be. Feeling God within me now is powerful. I also know that all of us need to have faith in this belief to help us through the darkest days... into the light.

My aim for this book is to help you realize that you are the creators of your life. I would like you to think about one thing you can take away from this book to assist you with your healing. I want to connect with you on a soul level. I will be sharing my teachings with you in the second part of this book, which is all about healing and techniques for a better quality of life, especially for those who have experienced abuse and trauma.

Chapter X: Therapy and a New Beginning

Gifts from Marie, My Therapist

I mentioned having therapy earlier. My cousin Anita kindly introduced me to Marie, who helped me so much through my darkest days. I have to thank her for her patience and kindness. She introduced me to a different spirituality, teaching me Reiki, the Japanese technique for stress reduction and relaxation, promoting healing in both body and mind. She showed me compassion as she listened to my life story. Marie also inspired me to seek recovery through meditation and to become mindful. We also discussed trauma and how it might have physically changed my brain patterns.

I learned that from a scientific perspective, the amygdala becomes over-activated when trauma has occurred. If this happens in childhood, the trauma may carry on into adulthood, to be acted out, or retreat internally. As you have seen from my story, I chose to act out my trauma. Our brains are malleable, especially when we are young children—the pathways mold and change as we grow and develop. The ability for this to happen is called 'neuroplasticity,' The brain's ability to adapt can also give a good therapist the tools that he or she needs to begin helping those who have suffered trauma.

According to scientific research undertaken in 2016, there are three phases of neuroplasticity, or the brain's ability to reorganize itself in forming new neural connections. After a trauma, neurons within the brain begin to die. This phase lasts for one or two days, and it uncovers secondary neural networks. These are the pathways that can help hide the trauma and teach our brains to retreat, which then changes our personalities. The mind can continue to change after this and open up new pathways for healing. The effects will, however, stay with us, unless we begin therapy or another healing practice as soon as possible after the traumatic event. If this doesn't happen, the brain will continue to change and create a "new" personality.

We usually have a fight-or-flight response when we experience a physical or emotional trigger. We remember our trauma, and it is real. Our brain is letting us know that we are hurting and that we need help. Therapy is focused on helping people realize that we don't bring the trauma upon ourselves, and we can take steps to heal from its harming influences. Getting through any trauma involves talking about our pain and processing what has happened to us.

Marie helped me to talk about my sexual abuse as a child, my physical and sexual abuse as an adult, and to talk about why traumatic situations have carried on finding me. We discussed why my relationships failed and why they were continual with bad or troubled men. My trauma therapy with Marie helped me to face the reality of the past, without getting stuck in it. Reducing my symptoms, we worked towards shifting focus from the past to the present and improving my daily functioning. I learned to reclaim my power because of her help and overcome the addictions associated with traumatic stress. I am continuing to refine the skills I need to prevent me from relapsing into making faulty decisions and getting into poor relationships, or from someone who cannot seem to stay away from the trauma itself.

VICTIM 2 VICTOR

The Tools Marie Gave to Me

Through Marie's training, I became a Tera Mai Seichem Reiki Masters healer. Reiki is administered through the laying on of one's hands and is based on the premise that there is a life force energy flowing through all of us. Reiki is this energy. When someone has low energy, we often get sick or feel stressed. If our Reiki is high, we are happy and healthy. When I discovered this, I realized that I had found the answer for many of my difficulties. It is a natural, safe, and simple method of spiritual healing or self-improvement. Anyone can use Reiki. It is useful in helping us through illness, sickness, trauma, and abuse. It can also be used in conjunction with other therapies and relaxation techniques to release stress and promote recovery. I went through the three training levels of Reiki to become a Reiki Master. It has been added to my skills as a yoga teacher, and I now have the tools to heal myself and help others.

Trauma has many physical effects, and it's vital to move beyond talking to a therapist when trying to heal. Even though talking is about healing, it doesn't always make our bodies realize that we are safe. Yoga is an excellent method of resetting our lives. It helps us in bringing our body and mind together, for us to be still. It allows us to feel everything and tolerate sensations while we live in the present and move away from what may be happening to us. I used yoga in conjunction with my therapy sessions as well as Reiki. It made talking about my life a little easier. A gentle and trauma-sensitive yoga practice gave me the opportunity of experiencing a change in my mental state. I shifted from always feeling stressed to being more relaxed. Yoga is non-verbal. The body is used as a means of self-expression, while the simple act of moving in conjunction with your body is in itself, healing.

Reiki and yoga have given me the strength to carry on, allowing the past and the present to flow from me so that I am now a more thoughtful and complete person.

Anu Verma

I Also Discovered Tony Robbins

As I mentioned earlier, I also began following Tony Robbins, a master in personal development. I attended the *Unleash the Power Within and Date with Destiny* seminars, and again his *Wealth and Life Mastery* courses. Attending his seminars was a significant investment for me, but it was the best one I could have made. There was no better way to spend my money. Tony Robbins' mission is to help individuals and businesses succeed. He is an entrepreneur, a bestselling author, a philanthropist, and the world's number one life and business strategist. Tony has helped more than fifty million people for over thirty years to find themselves and take their lives to another level. It doesn't matter how successful or unsuccessful you are; he can provide a breakthrough in the areas that matter the most, including our business, personal finances, intimate relationships, families, health, and career. He shares his viewpoints, techniques, and other practices in books, seminars, and speeches. He believes strongly in helping people improve their lives. He talks about various human needs, influences that affect people, the power of making decisions, and the necessity of achieving emotional mastery.

When I started listening to him talk about his life and work, I had little direction. I didn't believe in myself. I had so many questions, and Tony seemed to have all the answers that I needed. He taught me how to make wise decisions. He gave me strategies and techniques to achieve my goals. His influence shifted my focus from the bad that was going on around me to a better and brighter future. His advice and strategies are highly effective. They work. Strangely, what he taught seemed so simple afterward. All I had to do was to apply what he had said. Once I took his advice to heart, I began to find myself and pull all of my teaching and therapies together. His seminars made me feel enthusiastic and excited. My life changed because of Tony Robbins. I changed how I thought, as well as my beliefs and values. I was already on a path of personal development, and his help was invaluable in taking my journey to the next level.

He gave me the impetus to improve and to learn self-mastery. To take control of who I am and where I was going. I resonate deeply with his teachings. His seminars gave me the insight that I needed into what drives every decision, which I make, what my needs are, what my beliefs are about myself, and what my values are in life. He made me realize that I needed to take care of myself before I could heal or take care of others. He also helped me to reset my beliefs, to get rid of my limiting beliefs, which gave me back my self-worth and my self-esteem. I discovered that if I had negative thoughts about myself, it impacted on everything that I did and influenced every decision that I made.

I learned that it was only through self-reflection and turning to my spiritual side via meditation and deep inner work that I could realize my true potential and the gifts which I had been given. He said that if my expectations were turned into appreciation, the world would change immediately. This made me realize that most of my actions and thought patterns were based upon the old belief system which I held. This was based on one man who told me that I was not worthy of true love or happiness. I had avoided real life by working long hours, running frantically, escaping to foreign countries, and always being on the go. I didn't allow myself to stop or to smell the roses. Quite simply, I didn't know how to live in the present or in the best way possible.

Part II: Abuse and Trauma

Chapter I: Abuse

Abuse is defined as any action that intentionally harms or injures another person. It is the improper use or treatment of something, to unfairly or improperly gain benefit. It can come in many forms: physical or verbal abuse, injury assault, violation, rape, and unjust practices. Abuse also comes from other types of aggression. The psychological damage it causes can be complicated to heal, even more so than bodily harm.

Survivors often have intense, negative feelings long after the abuse has ended. Flashbacks, anxiety, and trust issues are common in those who have experienced this. It affects their ability to form relationships and to find happiness, and yet the effect of abuse doesn't have to be permanent. Therapists can help survivors stop harmful behaviors. However, the individual has to want to make this change. The World Health Organization lists several types of abuse, which will be explained next.

Physical Abuse

Physical abuse is defined as any intentional act that causes injury or trauma to another person. Children are often victims of physical abuse, but adults can also be. Adult physical abuse often comes in the form of domestic violence or workplace aggression.

Physical abuse results in several different types of injuries, including:

- Bruises, blisters, burns, scratches, and cuts
- Internal injuries and brain damage
- Broken bones, sprains
- Emotional and psychological harm
- Lifelong injury, even death.

The following signs of physical abuse may be seen by a teacher, caretaker, or someone who is interacting with a child:

- Visible and severe injuries
- Injuries to different areas of the body
- Different phases of healing
- Unexplained signs, or explained in a way that doesn't make sense
- The distinctive shape of the injury
- Frequency, timing, and history of injuries.

Child abuse usually results in the child experiencing the following symptoms of abuse:

- Aggression toward peers and pets
- Fear of parents or adults
- Withdrawal, depression, anxiety
- Wearing a long-sleeved garment out of season
- Nightmares and insomnia
- Immaturity, acting out, emotional or behavioral extremes,
- Self-destructive behavior or attitudes

VICTIM 2 VICTOR

Child and Adult Sexual Abuse

Sexual abuse is when a child is forced to participate in unwanted, unsafe, or degrading sexual activity. It includes rape and sexual assault—vaginal, oral, or anal.

Sexual abuse of children includes the following:

- Non-contact abuse
- Making a child view a sexual act
- Making a child look at or show sexual organs
- Inappropriate sexual talk
- Using sex toys, broken glass, bottles, or forcing the child to have sexual activity in a way that will hurt him or her
- Fondling and oral sex
- Contact abuse
- Penetration
- Making children perform a sexual act
- Exploitation
- Child pornography and prostitution

Signs of sexual abuse in a child include:

- Painful sitting, walking, and bowel problems
- Torn, stained, or bloody undergarments
- Bleeding, bruising, pain, and swelling of the genital area
- Frequent urinary tract or yeast infections
- Sexually transmitted diseases
  The child may experience emotional problems which include:
- A refusal to change clothes
- Being withdrawn, depressed, and anxious
- Eating disorders, and preoccupation with his or her body
- Aggression, delinquency, poor peer relationships

- Low self-image, poor self-care, lack of confidence
- Sudden absenteeism in school-age children and a decline in performance at school
- Substance abuse, running away, suicide attempts
- Sleep disturbances, fear of bedtime, nightmares, and bedwetting at an advanced age
- Sexual acting out, or excessive masturbation
- Unusual or repetitive soothing behaviors
- Sexual behaviors, or knowledge of sex that is unusual

Psychological Abuse

Psychological abuse can involve name-calling, continual insults, shaming, humiliation, hurtful sarcasm, constant criticism, screaming, and shouting. It can also be apparent when the child is rejected or ignored, being told that he or she is unwanted or unloved, and little interest being shown in him or her. Abuse also occurs in blaming, insulting, punishing by threatening abandonment, harm, or death. A child can become emotionally hurt when he or she is set up for failure, as this takes advantage of reliance on adults.

The physical signs of psychological abuse in a child include:

- Delays in development and wetting the bed
- Speech disorders
- Health problems like ulcers and skin disorders
- Obesity and weight fluctuations
- Sucking, biting, rocking
- Learning disabilities and developmental delays
- Overly compliant, or defensive
- Extreme emotions, aggression, or withdrawal
- Anxieties, phobias, and sleep disorder
- Destructive or anti-social behavior
- Inappropriate behavior
- Suicidal thoughts

Psychological abuse is also called emotional abuse and is a form of subjecting another to actions that can result in mental trauma. Linking it to anxiety, stress, chronic depression, or Post-Traumatic Stress Disorder (PTSD.) It is associated with situations in which there is a power imbalance between people.

Neglectful Abuse

Neglect is a form of abuse that results from the caregiver who is responsible for someone else's welfare but fails in that duty. Neglectful abuse can be a result of carelessness, unwillingness, indifference, or forgetfulness.

There are four types of neglect regarded as abuse:

- **Physical neglect**. Lack of food, shelter, or clothing is a visible form of negligence. If a child does not get enough to eat, then their primary need for nourishment is neglected.
- **Medical neglect**. A parent's failure to give the child medical or dental care. It can also occur when a parent does not allow the child to have vaccinations or medical care for severe illness—often resulting in death before the circumstances are discovered.
- **Educational neglect.** When the caregiver fails to provide for a child's needs concerning schooling or education, this is a crime in the United Kingdom. The offender may be prosecuted for the criminal offense of child abuse.
- **Emotional neglect.** When we think of abandonment, being left behind may come to mind, but that is not the only form of abuse under this heading. Emotional abuse happens when parents or caretakers are physically present but emotionally absent. This affects the child's self-esteem. Studies have shown that the younger a

child is when this emotional neglect occurs, the more damaging it becomes in adulthood.

Domestic Violence and Abuse

Domestic violence is a dreadful form of abuse. It takes a toll on both the victim and anyone else who is present. Even if the child is not the one who is being abused, watching an act of domestic violence can cause him or her to become traumatized and mentally abused. According to research, children exposed to domestic violence have a higher rate of behavioral, emotional, and societal problems. This can result in long and short-term effects that have an impact on the child's development.

When I wrote this book, there were more than three million reports of child abuse being made every year in the United States alone. It was an epidemic, and I don't believe that it is any better now. There is no doubt about the trauma and anguish which domestic violence brings when adults are involved. Domestic violence (DV), as it's sometimes known, includes dating violence, intimate partner abuse, and other types of violent action. Verbal or emotional violence that may occur when the perpetrator uses words to criticize, decrease the confidence of another, demean, or cause emotional harm. It has become a significant public health problem and affects millions of people. At times, it can even lead to death.

Domestic abuse statistics concerning those affected by intimate partner abuse were shocking. It was affecting between three and five percent of adult relationships, and this figure included two million women. Domestic abuse disproportionately affected women. It was believed that around one-third of women could expect to be the victim of domestic violence at some time in their life. In 2003, over thirteen hundred deaths were attributed to this, and that figure has since grown.

Chapter II: What is Sexual Abuse?

I am interested now to know what drives someone to abuse a child sexually. I want to understand what makes them a pedophile, and there aren't any easy answers other than the typical characteristics of an abuser. Someone who has power or influence over a child develops a sexual interest in them and acts on their selfish sexual fantasies and impulses. They don't have any internal constraints to stop them from betraying the child's trust or abusing them sexually. It's a dangerous form of power.

Sexual abuse is defined as sexual behaviors or a sex act forced upon a man, woman, or a child without their consent. Sex abuse is an act of violence that is used against someone who the abuser feels is weaker than them. It may come from an uncontrollable sex drive, but more often than not, it is a crime committed deliberately to control the victim.

Types of sexual assault or abuse include:

- **Incest** - Sexual abuse at the hands of a family member.

- **Rape** - Insertion of a body organ or an object into the sex organ of a woman or child with consent.

- **Sodomy** - Insertion of a body organ or other object into a person's anus or mouth without their consent.

Trauma and abuse are destructive, and according to therapists, the idea of "what doesn't kill you makes you stronger" side to trauma is challenging to understand, but it is essential. If you have faced adversity in your life, the very fact that you seek therapy means you are resourceful enough and want to overcome your trauma. The critical part of overcoming trauma is learning how to get rid of old traumatic patterns and learning to live with the best of both worlds. The resilience of someone who overcomes trauma, plus the optimism and mental freedom it takes to live a productive and successful life, will take you far.

Reports indicated that sixty percent of all people had some form of abuse or trauma in their childhood. This figure included sexual abuse, which in children was as high as one in five girls and one in twenty boys, making child sex abuse prolific. If you have experienced childhood sexual abuse, you may have a huge block in your mind that keeps you from improving or managing your life and making the right decisions. Your childhood sexual abuse is always in the back of your mind, and little things can trigger memories and thoughts of that abuse. Even if you don't consciously think about it, the abuse you experienced as a child can bring feelings of worthlessness and pain. You either become manic in your actions to combat these subliminal thoughts, or you become withdrawn and antisocial.

Abuse is difficult to bring up in conversation. You don't often hear people talking about their childhood abuse as if it were a common occurrence. Sadly, due to this topic not being widely spoken about, it makes it difficult for sufferers to learn about how to heal from abuse, how to uncover it, face it, feel the pain associated with it, and then to let it go.

The most challenging part of healing from abuse is often reaching out and getting help. In our culture, we are taught to tolerate difficult experiences by "pulling ourselves up by our bootstraps" and just dealing with the experience. We are prepared to be self-sufficient and to handle our problems. Our self-reliant attitude makes it very difficult to request help from a therapist or an outsider or even our own families.

Not discussing the abuse is cultural. It is so overwhelming to you that your brain seeks to bury it. You don't want to face it, so you push it down or rationalize it and try to continue with your life. Repressing memories might work in the short term. Still, long-term, buried abuse can impact your stress response, decrease your emotional regulation, cause chronic cortisol release, and bring up coping behaviors that ultimately hurt you in the long term.

Childhood Sexual Abuse

Sexual abuse at any time, but especially in childhood, is a sinister type of trauma. It instills shame in the victim, and childhood sexual abuse victims are usually too young to know how to express what has happened to them. They don't know how to seek help, and unfortunately, they are easily persuaded that what happened to them was "okay." However, when not adequately treated, childhood sexual abuse can result in a lifetime of PTSD, depression, anxiety, destructive behaviors, and unsatisfactory relationships.

The World Health Organization has formally recognized the existence of complex post-traumatic stress disorder as a condition that survivors of childhood abuse suffer. It is different from other forms of PTSD, and sufferers often have wholly pervasive and rigid negative beliefs about themselves.

Often, sexually abused children struggle with managing their feelings; they have a hard time trusting others and often have feelings of shame and inadequacy. The Truth Project found that eighty-five of the participants in the study had mental problems in later life. These health issues included depression and anxiety and severe struggles with education or in getting a job. Four out of ten participants in the trial had difficulties with relationships and most avoided sexual intimacy. Others had multiple sexual partners. Many of the participants were dependent on alcohol, had trouble sleeping or eating, and one out of five participants in the study had tried to kill themselves.

An even more disturbing statistic has shown that survivors of childhood sexual abuse are at considerable risk of heart disease and cancer. Years of chronic stress and trying to overcome their past sexual abuse can cause health problems.

Sexual abuse, molestation, and rape are shame-filled events that our culture tends to suppress, and we hide that these events even happened. As a result, there is very little information about sexual abuse, and we all gasp when we hear about it on the news. Fortunately, therapists, families, and even the victims themselves realize that childhood sexual abuse is a problem that requires a solution.

The website *childtrauma.org* states that one out of three females and one out of five males in the United States are victims of sexual abuse before eighteen. In the United Kingdom, police have recorded six thousand childhood rapes in under eighteens, and over six thousand, two hundred violations of under sixteen. The years 2016-17 saw two thousand, eight hundred, and forty-five documented sexual abuse problems against children in Wales. The statistics go on and on. No country in the world is immune from child sexual abuse. The sad caveat to this story is that most children are victimized by someone whom they know well.

Childhood sexual abuse affects children across every ethnic, educational, religious, socioeconomic, and regional line. There is no discrimination in childhood sexual abuse.

Child sexual abuse is so widespread that it has become a public health problem with the potential to undermine the healthy psychosocial development of children and adolescents.

VICTIM 2 VICTOR

Unfortunately, childhood as well as adult victims of sexual abuse, try to downplay their experiences. They claim that it never happened or that it "wasn't that bad."

Small children who are victims are often told to keep it quiet; 'it was a fun game,' or 'how we show that we love each other.' These children don't fully understand what was done to them. They do know that the sexual abuse which was performed on them was wrong, painful, and shameful.

Survivors of sexual abuse need to know that it is essential to realize that abuse comes in many colors, sizes, and shapes, and all of it is bad.

The most common effect of childhood sexual abuse is Post Traumatic Stress Disorder (PTSD). Symptoms extend into adulthood and include withdrawn behaviors, reenactments of the traumatic event, avoiding circumstances that remind children of the event, and physiological hyperreactivity.

Children abused at an early age often become hyper-sexualized or sexually reactive. They have issues with promiscuity and low self-esteem. These feelings can lead to substance abuse. It is reported that 90% of patients in the addiction field of alcohol, drugs, and eating disorders have a known history of some form of abuse.

The American Academy of Experts in Traumatic Stress (AAETS) goes on to stress that specific symptoms of sexual abuse are:

- Withdrawal and mistrust of adults
- Thoughts of suicide
- Difficulty in relating to others except in sexual or seductive ways
- Unusual interest in or avoidance of all things sexual or physical
- Frequent accidents or self-injurious behaviors
- Secretiveness or unusual aggressiveness
- Sexual components to drawings and games

- Neurotic reactions including obsessions, phobias, and compulsive behaviors
- Habit disorders like cutting or biting themselves or others, fighting, general misbehaviors
- Unusual sexual knowledge
- Prostitution
- Forcing sexual acts on other children
- Extreme fear of being touched
- Unwillingness to submit to physical examination

Children who have experienced sexual abuse will recover much faster and let go of the symptoms if they have a supportive, caring adult, particularly a parent who is regularly in their life. A parent that understands, nurtures, listens, and ultimately takes a child to therapy can help decrease or prevent PTSD symptoms.

It is interesting to note that thirty-five percent of child sexual abusers were once abused. With support and counseling, it may help to reduce the possibility of a victim repeating this sexually abusive pattern.

The light at the end of the tunnel? Not every survivor of childhood abuse ends badly, and their "fates are not set in stone." The government in the United Kingdom set up the Truth Project's Independent Inquiry into Child Sexual Abuse. Bryony Farrant, the project's chief psychologist, believes that our brain's plasticity enables us all to repair and to reconstruct ourselves so that we can fully recover and live a fruitful life.

Adult Sexual Abuse

The definition of sexual assault is broad; it includes everything from rape to an unwelcome hand gesture on parts of the body. Sexual abuse is becoming an epidemic and is a significant health problem. Even in adults, any form of sexual violence, including rape, molestation, and other forms of non-consensual sexual contact, is abuse. Those who have investigated and studied sexual abuse agree that abuse from one adult to another is never about sex. It is often an attempt to gain power over others.

Assistance after a sexual assault can be invaluable and save lives. If you are a victim of any type of rape, including drug or date rape, you need to call local police or seek help and make sure that you have received a hospital or medical examination.

Rape

Rape or forced sexual contact is with someone who does not consent. Forcing sex upon someone who does not want it, who is intoxicated or not legally old enough to give consent, is rape. Any form of forcible sexual contact can have long-lasting effects on an abused person. Forcible sex brings on trauma and causes the brain to change in several ways.

According to new research, sexual and emotional abuse affect regions that are involved in self-awareness, and sexual abuse mainly affects areas involved in genital sensation.

The brain alters patterns of signaling from the usual pathways to cope with overwhelming experiences of trauma. These pathways are no longer used and exercised, and they thin and become stagnant from lack of use.

If the abuse was sexual, there are changes in the somatosensory cortex or the area that processes sensations and perceptions. Somatosensory areas create a map of the body and the brain and each region processes feelings. Women who were sexually abused have thinning in the area where the genitalia was inserted.

Many sexual abuse survivors reported problems in adulthood with sex. These included a reduction in desire and sensation and often genital pain. Some studies suggest that the thinning of the cortex is associated with a lowered pain threshold. You would ultimately feel pain instead of touch in that area. The result? Sexually abused adults find that they have no sensations when having sex and their sex drives are drastically altered. Some become manic in having sex to find satisfaction, while others become cold and unfeeling.

No type of abuse in childhood or adulthood is acceptable. The type of emotional and physical trauma that abuse causes on the brain wave changes make life miserable.

I am a survivor and have risen above my childhood sexual abuse. It hasn't been easy, and I lost myself along the way, but I did it, and so can you.

Chapter III: What is Trauma?

I could not heal entirely without knowing about the types of trauma that I had experienced. By giving a name to them, I was able to work with my therapist to find the best way for me to heal. It was difficult because I had experienced so many different traumas and abuse throughout my life. Most of my relationships had caused me significant distress, and my trauma count increased until I couldn't make the right decisions or be happy.

I would like now to give you the medical and scientific definitions of trauma and abuse. I hope that doing this will help you to begin your healing process.

What is Trauma?

Trauma that begins in childhood can continue to affect us well into adulthood. Continuing feelings of shame and guilt, disconnection, and inability to relate to others can cause emotional stagnation. Also, difficulty in controlling our emotions, giving us heightened anxiety and depression. We may become angry and unable to trust others, always having a sense of loneliness and isolation. The dictionary definition is of a deeply distressing or disturbing experience, which overwhelms our ability to cope.

Trauma also causes feelings of helplessness, diminishes the sense of self, and the ability to feel a full range of emotions in enjoying experiences. When defined in this way, is it any wonder that we aren't all traumatized to the point of indecision? Trauma is also believed to be an emotional response to terrible events that can happen at any point in our lives after any traumatic event like an accident, rape, or abuse. Even a natural disaster, shock, and denial are typical. Longer-term reactions include unpredictable emotions, flashbacks, strained relationships, and physical symptoms like headaches and nausea.

Trauma can also come from illness or disease, accidents, grief, divorce, genocide, torture, and war. We can also cause trauma to ourselves by performing random actions and the guilt associated with these actions. Trauma does not discriminate. It can happen to anyone, irrespective of where any of us are in the world.

When I wrote this book, The National Center for Mental Health Promotion and Youth Violence Prevention reported that twenty-five percent of children had witnessed or had been involved in a traumatic event. This included 'sexual abuse trauma' before they were just four years old. It isn't easy to face the pain that you experienced because of childhood sexual abuse. You don't have the tools or the emotional or mental maturity to process what happened to you. The inability to understand this trauma causes the child to experience unresolved traumatic stress, panic attacks, and episodes of depression when they can't seem to let go of the events that happened in the past. Memories and suppressed memories of physical and sexual abuse or other childhood trauma can interfere with everyday life as an adult, making it necessary to face up to these issues.

The body and our mind keep a record of all of our past traumas. Trauma is stored in thoughts and memories and is located in cells, muscles, and tissues of our physical bodies. Traumatic experiences are visceral. They overpower our senses and leave us with memories. Science has shown that the effects of trauma are visible in abnormal EEGs or brain scans.

If we find ourselves having a difficult time in interpersonal relationships, and that we are unable to be happy with anyone, then therapy can help us to heal. I have also found self-help programs and alternative holistic treatments hugely beneficial during my healing.

Naming Your Trauma

None of us fit into one specific trauma. What we go through in life often is a combination of many different traumas, but if we know the types of trauma which we have suffered, this gives us power over memories and thoughts.

Acute Stress Disorder

Acute stress disorder is severe anxiety, dissociation, and other symptoms within one month after exposure to a traumatic event. This can include witnessing a death, a severe accident, rape, or seeing someone hurt. It is labeled as a mental health condition that can occur immediately after a traumatic event. It can cause different psychological symptoms and, without treatment, often leads to post-traumatic stress disorder, as I mentioned earlier in the book.

Treatment can include being prescribed anti-anxiety medication, selective serotonin reuptake inhibitors, and antidepressants. Cognitive-behavioral therapy (CBT) may help with recovery and prevent the onset of PTSD.

Post-Traumatic Stress Disorder (PTSD)

Therapists and medical doctors explained that I had experienced a trauma and that I was suffering from PTSD. As a child, I had been unable to cope with this or the feelings which it caused. My sense of self was damaged, and I had tried to shut myself down emotionally in an attempt to survive. PTSD often develops when someone goes through a terrifying event or ordeal, which causes or threatens them with physical harm. My dark thoughts were persistent and frightening. The memory of what my relative had done was always in my thoughts.

The symptoms of PTSD also included avoiding any situations that would cause me to recall the traumatic event. So, I had problems sleeping, and I was afraid to be alone. I still experience flashbacks of how it felt when Gary and a relative were abusing me. I understand that acting impulsively or aggressively can be another symptom that an abused child might suffer. I, fortunately, wasn't aggressive, but I did act impulsively, which caused my family to be alarmed by my behavior.

If symptoms of severe trauma last for more than a month and affect our ability to function, PTSD may be diagnosed. It's interesting to note that some people who have PTSD may not have shown any symptoms for months or even years. Combat veterans, and those involved in natural disasters, can find themselves dealing with the symptoms for the rest of their lives. PTSD is a mental health disorder that often occurs in the aftermath of situations that involve violence or physical harm, or an imminent threat of this. During everyday life, our brain is relatively calm, but when exposed to a traumatic event, it will switch the body from survival mode to a state of restoration. PTSD occurs when that switch doesn't happen, leaving the survivor in a constant state of emergency.

The Freedom K9 Project, in Indiana, trains service dogs to help survivors overcome the symptoms of PTSD. They reported that seven out of ten psychologically abused women developed PTSD. The veterans who returned from war also had PTSD because of the death and violence which they had experienced. Due to the world's involvement in combat situations during the twenty-first century, PTSD is commonly associated with the direct experience of wartime conditions. Between eleven and twenty out of every one hundred veterans in the United States of America, or around twenty percent of those who served in wartime, will have PTSD in any given year. Why is this percentage so high? Veterans live through traumatic events that cause them to fear for their lives. Terrible things may happen directly in front of them, and they feel helpless. The intense emotions caused by wartime events create changes in the brain. Conversely, not every veteran will develop PTSD, and there isn't any apparent reason why this is the case.

The disorder is also prevalent in the aftermath of kidnappings, floods, train wrecks, car accidents, civilian bombings, and rapes. Similarly, child sexual abuse, and without help or therapy, these symptoms can last for years. Child sexual abuse (CSA) can involve many activities that purposefully expose children to adult sexual behaviors and perspectives. Acts involving groping, genital contact, or intercourse are all part of the molestation. Children don't understand the sexual perspectives and actions of adults, so any intentional exposure to these aspects of adult life can produce trauma. The most traumatic forms of CSA typically involve a violent or extreme invasion of physical space repeatedly occurring for months or even years, which often happens at the hands of close family members.

A child can develop PTSD responses to any type, degree, or frequency of sexual abuse. According to the American Academy of Child & Adolescent Psychiatry, PTSD in young children manifests differently. Symptoms can include losing interest in activities that bring joy or pleasure and acting out in some form, the behaviors committed against them. PTSD symptoms also include regressing to age-inappropriate behaviors like bedwetting or thumb sucking. Developing unusual fears about early death, refusing to talk, or having an incredibly strong attachment to authority figures such as parents or teachers. PTSD also often brings on learning problems that cause difficulties in school or groups. Symptoms found in older sexually abused children and teenagers may include disrespectful attitudes toward authority figures, often leading to disruptive and damaging actions.

There are definite links between physically invasive CSA and PTSD. It is, however, impossible to predict which abused child will develop trauma-related symptoms, even in the aftermath of identical forms of abuse. Child sexual abuse victims who develop the disorder can experience different symptoms of varying degrees of severity. Children who suffer from child sexual abuse-related post-traumatic stress disorder can recover with the help of treatment. This requires loving care, a dynamic therapist, and social understanding.

More Symptoms of PTSD

Think about the last time you were terrified to the point of fight or flight. These are the other symptoms that those who have PTSD can exhibit:

Re-Experiencing

- Flashbacks
- Nightmares
- An unfavorable change in beliefs or feelings
- Loss of loving feelings
- Forgetting part of the traumatic event, or not being able to talk about it
- Feeling like the world is a dangerous place
- No one is trustworthy

Hyper-Arousal

- Avoidance behavior
- Inability to sleep or relax
- Finding it difficult to concentrate
- Being easily startled
- Often living internally

Psychological Trauma

Psychological trauma is defined as damage to the mind due to a distressing or a traumatic event. The trauma creates an overwhelming amount of stress that exceeds our ability to cope with it mentally. Psychological trauma causes feelings of fear and anxiety. Sufferers often experience the trauma repeatedly. Some triggers cause the recollection of memories. Fortunately, these episodes can occur less frequently over time.

Psychological trauma can also cause emotional fluctuations, unhappiness, anxiety, loneliness, irritability, and anger. It can lead to acting out, manic behavior, hiding, or drawing ourselves inward. Psychological trauma often affects how a child or an adult handles pain, and it overwhelms the ability to cope with experiences rationally. It causes impaired feelings and decreases the sense of self. There are no set criteria that determine the causes of this. However, circumstances of psychological trauma include loss of control, acts of terrorism, abuse, suffering, and uncertainty.

The symptoms appear differently in every sufferer, but some common ones do exist. Emotional signs include anger, denial, sadness, disgrace, anguish, and intense feelings of guilt. Sufferers may also experience psychological problems such as depression, anxiety, dissociative disorder, or substance abuse. These were symptoms that I experienced throughout my life.

Looking back now, I can see that I was angry at myself, my family, and everyone around me. I felt sadness and anguish. My feelings of guilt led me to make unwise decisions. I was depressed, suicidal, and experimented with drugs. I also drank alcohol to excess. All the while hoping these harmful remedies would stop me from being able to feel anything.

Chronic Tension

Trauma causes the brain to activate the fight or flight response. My mind, more often than not, turned to the flight state. I left on airplanes for different parts of the world to try to escape from my trauma. I took up white water rafting, bungee jumping, and did all types of extreme activities, and I also worked hard in my career; all of this was to help me get rid of the feelings of unworthiness, guilt, fear, and sadness that I was experiencing. Travel, work, and extreme activities became my escape from trauma.

Social Withdrawal

Research into childhood trauma reveals that trauma leads to Social Anxiety Disorder (SAD). Sexual abuse, and the feeling of not being cared for or loved and nurtured, are directly related to SAD. I felt an intense, persistent fear of being watched and judged by others. I looked at every relationship that I had with skepticism, anxiety, and the thought that the relationship would inevitably turn out ugly. The social withdrawal was one of the symptoms which I had during my relationship with Paul. I was always checking where he was and how he acted around other girls. I accused him of having an affair on innumerable occasions because I couldn't learn to trust.

Psychological trauma is also linked to PTSD. This type of injury involves persistent and frightening thoughts or memories of the abuse and how we could have stopped it. Strong feelings of guilt enter our minds, as we wonder what we could have done differently. Those who have experienced traumatic events may have difficulty adjusting and coping. This is together with recurrent, unwanted, and distressing memories of those traumatic events as well as flashbacks, upsetting dreams, or nightmares. This may also lead to severe emotional distress or physical reactions.

Psychological trauma following an evil act perceived by our nervous system to be life-threatening involves the weakening of cognitive, emotional, adaptive, physical, spiritual, and social abilities. Psychological trauma affects the ability to process thoughts and to make sound judgments. It appears in our emotions, like shame, guilt, fear, anger, and pain. Psychological trauma affects our view of the world and how we see reality. The understanding and meaning life, society, and our spiritual thoughts are also our relationships with spouses, family, friends, and colleagues.

Developmental Trauma

In the first five years of life, children need safe, predictable, accessible, and loving caretakers. In a caring environment, the brain usually develops as healthy and normal. When a child experiences stress such as neglect, physical or sexual abuse, and for an extended period, the sequential development of the brain is disturbed. It still develops, but some foundational steps are missing. Many emotions, thought patterns, and memories are out of order.

Children who are unable to find a sense of stability, and control, become helpless. They are unable to grasp what is going on and can't do anything about what is happening. In their minds, they go from being fearful of the fight to a flight and freeze response. When they are exposed to reminders of a trauma, they tend to act it out as if it was happening again. Sensations, sounds, images, situations can all be triggers that take the child back into their trauma. Many of the later problems experienced by traumatized children can be understood to lessen the perceived threat. Caregivers, parents, teachers, and others don't always understand this, which leads to the child being labeled as oppositional, rebellious, antisocial, or unmotivated.

According to *Psychology Today*, the brain develops from the bottom up. The lower parts are responsible for responding to stress and in ensuring survival, while the upper portions are necessary for making sense of what we are experiencing. The upper portions are responsible for ensuring how we use and pass moral judgment about others, how we respond to circumstances, relating to others, and becoming part of society. Think about the brain as a ladder. The growth of the upper parts is dependent on the healthy development of the lower section. If stress responses occur over an extended period, many steps in the development of the brain are missing, and similarly, the rungs of the ladder.

Development trauma manifests itself in many ways, including sensory processing disorder, attention deficit hyperactivity disorder or ADHD, oppositional defiant disorder, bipolar, and other personality disorders. Psychologists believe that developmental trauma occurs in adults who "haven't grown up," or who are unaware that their actions are wrong.

As I reflect on the partners who I chose during my life journey, it is interesting now to be able to see that there may have been some form of developmental trauma. They didn't seem to know that what they were doing was wrong, and they certainly didn't regard themselves as being damaged in any way.

Vicarious Trauma

Vicarious trauma is a technical challenge for therapists. Those who work in law enforcement, emergency medical and fire services, or others with similar humanitarian occupations are often traumatized when hearing and reading about tragedies, even by responding to the aftermath of traumatic events on multiple occasions. Vicarious trauma can be described as the transformation which occurs in a trauma worker because of empathic engagement with traumatized clients and their reports of traumatic experiences. Those who are exposed to vicarious trauma respond in several ways. They can become more cynical or fearful. Children and adults who continually hear about friends or siblings being abused can also suffer trauma from this. It becomes hard to separate themselves from the victim, and they may begin to respond as if they were also being abused.

Historical or Intergenerational Trauma

An emotional and psychological injury caused by trauma and experienced by a large group over a long period is called 'historical' or 'intergenerational trauma.' Those who haven't directly gone through the trauma but have heard about it may become afraid that their lives will take a similar turn. Look at apartheid, genocide, slavery, war, and discrimination. The Holocaust was an extreme example that lived on in many people, long after the abuse stopped. Slavery is another trauma that is still experienced by many, and again, long after the actual slave trade was abolished.

Historical trauma, in simple terms, is the collective emotional harm suffered by a generation because of a traumatic experience or an event from the past. The symptoms and emotions of Intergenerational trauma come from perceived trauma and often manifests itself into high rates of alcoholism, depression, anxiety, and substance abuse within afflicted communities. Scientists have also tested the theory that trauma can leave a chemical mark on someone's genes, which is then passed down to later generations.

Complex Trauma

As a result of the ongoing abuse that I suffered from the age of three and throughout my early childhood, the continual exposure to these events eventually led to complex trauma. Complex trauma is the result of chronic and prolonged traumatic experiences and situations that are invasive and interpersonal. They have severe consequences arising from prolonged abuse or profound neglect.

Complex trauma often occurs early in childhood. It can disrupt many aspects of the brain's development, emotional structure, and the child's sense of self. A complex traumatic event is often perpetrated by someone we know, and the trauma that is caused can interrupt the child's ability to form secure attachments. It also frequently affects many aspects of an adult's healthy physical and mental development. The complex trauma that I suffered at the hands of my father's friend and a family member made it almost impossible for me to have a healthy relationship with men.

A child needs to learn to trust others, to regulate his or her emotions, and to interact with the world. Children quickly develop a sense of being safe or unsafe, as they come to understand their value as an individual. When complex trauma interrupts a child's life, they soon learn that they cannot rely on others to help them. As adults, those who suffered from complex trauma may go from person to person trying to find a safe-haven, and someone to care for them. Often this is very difficult, as I discovered. It is challenging for an abused child to grow up into an adult who can manage his or her own emotions, and it is easy to become overwhelmed. Just like I felt when suicide became my answer to depression and fear.

Chapter IV: Easing the Pain of Trauma

If you feel that you are at a stage in your life and you are ready to make a difference, there are steps you can take to survive a traumatic experience. As a small child, we might not follow them, but all that changes once we become adults. When we have been through stressful events or a series of events that happen to us or which we bring upon ourselves, we usually experience feelings of helplessness and horror. The physical challenges of serious injury, such as suicide, are also common.

We can help ourselves get through a traumatic experience without suffering from mental health problems, using abusive behaviors, or contemplating suicide. Here are a few suggestions of things that I found helpful in getting me through the emotional and physical trauma caused by my childhood abuse.

Don't Feel Isolated

Reaching out to friends and family will keep you from becoming or feeling isolated. Talking to others who had the same experiences as I did was extremely important. I realize how important it is to open these lines of communication as soon as possible. Having these conversations about my issues has been a significant part of my recovery.

Sexually abused children tend, unfortunately, to try to make themselves seem smaller or to hide away from loved ones. They don't want to talk to anyone, which causes them to become isolated. If a child who has been sexually abused is also threatened, he or she may not be able to talk about the experience—often being afraid that this will result in harm to family members or themselves. Threats and misunderstandings are hard shells to breakthrough!

When you live with the side effects of trauma as an adult, you can hide from anything social. If you avoid communication with others or continue to act out the trauma, I want you to know that you are not alone. When you have survived a traumatic event as an adult or as a child, you feel isolated. Some therapists can help with this in group therapy sessions, which can introduce you to other people who are in similar circumstances. You may also have loving family members who will finally understand your abuse issues.

Understand What Happened

An abused child will not know what to do or how to talk about their trauma, and they may act out of character. It's crucial to find the right time and the right place to speak and to be careful about the tone of voice, to listen, and to follow this up. Never blame, or judge. Children don't understand what is happening to them. They need to be reassured that what has happened to them wasn't their fault.

Communicate

Adults need to avoid bottling up their emotions. Trying to ignore or forget a traumatic event can cause even more significant emotional trauma. An essential part of recovery is learning to be okay with your memories of the traumatic event and the thoughts or events that can trigger these. Facing your feelings head-on is essential. You need to take care of these events in a way that helps you to move forward. Be kind to yourself. Talk to your family, friends, and colleagues about your trauma. Talking enables you to get over your feelings and face up to what has happened. Don't reject the support of other people or refuse their help.

Seek Professional Help

If you suspect sexual abuse has happened to your child or if you have undergone this yourself, find a Child Psychologist or a therapist who is experienced in handling abuse. They will know what to do and how to deal with the situation. Talk to a therapist and reveal your abuse issues. Several techniques can be used to help you to heal.

The stress that happens after a traumatic event can be emotionally and physically crippling. Sadness, depression, and grief can become an integral part of your daily life. If your feelings are as severe as this, they will interfere with your everyday life, and it's time to find a mental health expert who can help. Preferably a licensed mental health professional who has had training, supervision, and clinical experience working directly with trauma. He or she may be a Psychologist, licensed mental health counselor, or a social worker.

Exercise

Get out and about. Move around. Professionals believe that exercise and movement are among the most effective ways to handle the after-effects of a traumatic event. Try deep breathing, gentle stretching, and walking. Don't force things and rest if you are tired.

Low to moderate exercise elevates mood, reduces anxiety, and is an overall stress buffer. Exercise benefits those with PTSD and improves cardiovascular health, weight loss, and greater flexibility. Given the benefits of exercise, if you have experienced abuse and trauma or if you have PTSD, you need to get out and move. You will be all the better for it.

VICTIM 2 VICTOR

Listen to your body

You need to listen to what your body is telling you. Eat healthily, rest when you are tired, and do things that make you happy. Work toward a regular sleep schedule. Read. Do something with friends. Treat yourself. Most of all, don't give up! It is easy to stay in bed and pull the covers over your head, but you must try to resist this urge.

Stay Away from Drugs and Alcohol

Drinking or doing drugs to bring on sleep, or to take the edge from a traumatic event, is one of the worst things you can do. Trying to numb your emotions or to forget things may work in the short term, but drugs and alcohol can harm you in the long run. Addictions lead to mental and physical problems, and possibly even long-term dependence.

Research has shown that there is a strong link between traumatic events and substance use problems. People who have experienced child abuse, criminal assault, natural disasters, or other traumatic events may turn to alcohol or drugs. This helps them deal with their feelings, including emotional pain, bad memories, guilt, shame, and anxiety.

Once you start on the alcohol and drug abuse cycle, you are exposed to more traumatic events that promote even more abusive reactions, creating further trauma. It is a vicious circle and one I was in for many of my adult years until I found a way out. Trauma and substance problems don't only cause havoc physically and mentally, but these activities also create significant problems in relationships.

Get into a Routine

Ordinary life is usually interrupted by a traumatic event. It's essential to get past the stress or trauma of this and return to daily life as soon as possible to re-establish a sense of normality and to regain control—practice self-care routines after any trauma. Get more rest, find someone to talk to, and try to carry on with your daily tasks the same as you did before the traumatic event occurred.

Fix the Little Things

Take time to resolve the small conflicts in your life. If you have an enormous task to do, break it up into smaller tasks. Set priorities and tackle them when you can.

Find Engaging Hobbies

Developing new hobbies is an excellent self-care tool. You could try writing, art, gardening, sewing, knitting, photography, or any other hobby that interests you. The secret is to do something active that will take your mind away from your memories of the trauma.

Meditate

Meditation will keep your brain from thinking about stress because it turns you inwards. Deep breathing or focusing on your outward breath eases the mind. Focus your attention on parts of your body as you meditate. You might also like to repeat a mantra, pray, or do yoga. There are many meditations and self-help apps that you can download. Most of them are easy to follow. Helping you learn to be calm and to quieten your mind.

Celebrate life

Realize that it is good to feel happy and to celebrate success. Enjoy the warmth of your friendships and family after a traumatic event. For many years, I avoided family gatherings as I did not feel like I belonged, and I felt like an outsider, so I would make up any excuse not to attend parties and weddings. I realized once I had healed that attending family gatherings and parties should be positive experiences as they are loud and happy occasions, so they should be enjoyed. You need to join in, to recover your sense of what is normal.

Listen to Music

Studies have shown that music can reduce emotional stress induced by trauma. When we are dealing with arousal or intrusive symptoms, music can re-channel or redirect emotions. If you like it, any type of music is good for the soul. We can find inner peace and comfort when listening to our favorite genre of music. Music therapy has been used as a healing tool since the eighteenth century. It has helped victims who suffered trauma following physical abuse, terrorist attacks, war, asylum, mental abuse, and emotional and sexual abuse. Music is beneficial for those who have PTSD. Calming and soothing melodies can channel positive emotions and memories that are not associated with traumatic events.

Join a Support Group

Talking over what you are going through with others who have had the same experience can be helpful. Support groups give us a lift, which often includes advice on dealing with a particular trauma. Local support groups can be found online or through a mental health expert.

Anu Verma

Chapter V: Healing Trauma

Childhood, Adolescence, and Adulthood

As children, it is hard to distinguish feelings. We believe that we are our feelings. If our feelings are treated as acceptable in certain situations but not others, we may decide that these unacceptable feelings should be hidden. Healing from childhood trauma is necessary so that we can ground ourselves when we are adults. It is essential to complete the process that should have occurred when the incident caused us harm.

Reframing childhood memories can happen when we are in a safe environment and with someone whom we trust. It's possible then to go into detail about painful memories, talk them through, discuss what happened and how we currently feel. As we tell our story, our therapist or listener can interrupt to remind us to think about the details in our current environment, including the couch that we are sitting on, the lighting in the room, the pictures, textures, and other physical factors around us.

Throughout the telling of our story, we are weaving elements into it that have a safe context. Telling our story is one way of neutralizing and re-coding what was once a stressful thing, but which now includes elements of safety and security. So that in the next recalling, the memory will also include details and descriptions from the time when we described the story and thus links memories into a safe place.

VICTIM 2 VICTOR

There are a few steps to follow in adulthood to help us to heal from the trauma we may have experienced in our childhood:

- **Ground it.** To start with, be at one with your body. Find a comfortable place where you will not be disrupted. Sit in silence and shut your eyes. Breathe deeply and bring your awareness into the body. Relax your muscles. Feel connected to the ground. Imagine a flow of energy going from the tailbone towards the earth's core.

- **Recall it.** Think of something that may trigger an emotional reaction to an event from the past. Go through what has happened in as much depth as you can. Imagine as if you are in that time and location. Experience it again through all your senses. When emotions start playing their role, feel them.

- **Sense it.** Breathe in slowly, then relax. Mentally scan for any sensations on the body. Identify bodily trends like itchiness, pain, and stiffness. Each feeling you experience provides detailed information; you need to recall your previous experience. Start exploring these sensations and quietly explain them to yourself.

- **Name it.** When you've identified all of your physical reactions and have defined them, go on to name the trauma. If you connect a physical feeling with the emotion that you experience, this will help you to understand what's going on. Is that stiffness in the chest due to anxiety? Can you sense the fire of anger?

- **Love it.** You should welcome everything you feel whether that appears correct to your mind or not. You have to verbalize it too. The terms you use may mean that you admire yourself when you feel frustrated, depressed, and nervous. Follow the "love it" with any emotion that you experience, particularly the difficult ones. Accept your connection to humanity and respect yourself for doing it.

- **Feel and experience it.** Feel the sensations and emotional reactions. Allow the feelings to flow and work. It's the way. Don't attempt to alter them or to cover them up. Happily, accept any distress that you're feeling and knowing that it's going to go away eventually, and you will soon recover. Permit your body to react as it wishes or how it needs to. If you need to cry, then please do so. If you have the urge to shout or to hit anything, then you should call or punch the air. Share your thoughts productively, to help them to move, and to be able to process them fully.

- **Receive messages and wisdom.** Are the feelings you're experiencing now connected with feelings from your memories? You could be feeling emotionless currently. If this is the case, then question yourself, "If the emotion or sensation was going to tell me something, what would that be?" Try to write down your thoughts and emotions. Write about what the feeling means to you.

- **Share it.** Do this when you feel ready to share your feelings and thoughts with others. If you're still unclear, jot them down. Describe what feelings came about the first time the traumatic event happened. How you responded then and what you are feeling about this event now. Speaking about or trying to write about your feelings and experiences is a vital part of therapy.

- **Let it go.** Sit in silence and visualize the energy that your trauma has taken up inside your body. Implement a physical release ritual such as writing a letter to the person who upset you and then tearing the letter up or burning it. This may help you to let go of the pain and anger that you may be feeling. It would also help you to forgive and to allow space inside of you, which may have been taken up by the trauma. This space could then be filled with new positive energy that will help us to build a life that we love.

Healing emotional wounds is a process that will feel uncomfortable at first, but then the energy which has been consumed by the trauma will be released, making space for new positive energy that will help us to build a life that we love. The whole journey will be a rewarding and life-enhancing experience of healing old wounds and making space for love and light.

Types of Therapies

I will now discuss the various modes of therapy which can be used to heal the trauma.

EMDR or Eye Movement Desensitization and Reprocessing

VICTIM 2 VICTOR

EMDR involves focusing on a traumatic experience or our negative thoughts while visually tracking something moving in front of our eyes. There are many debates on whether eye movements have a place within the field of psychology. Nevertheless, the treatment is highly effective for the elimination of symptoms of trauma and other distress. Patients are safely taught to see images associated with the trauma such as self-thoughts, emotions, and body sensations. The key is to facilitate the natural healing process of the brain to come to an adaptive resolution.

EMDR is not about resolving difficulties. It is valuable in life-enhancing ways, removing the blocks which may inhibit healing and progress. It can help patients to feel more empowered and in charge of their lives. EMDR is a non-invasive and evidence-based method of psychotherapy that uses adaptive information processing. The therapy usually involves an eight-phase treatment that identifies and addresses experiences that have overwhelmed the brains' natural resilience or coping capacity.

Francine Shapiro, Ph.D., discovered by accident that emotional and behavioral symptoms resulting from trauma tended to resolve when the traumatized person allowed himself or herself to recall various aspects of memory; this occurred in bilateral stimulation, such as eye movements. Dr. Shapiro and her associates focused on several procedures to coordinate this dual awareness. The procedures were later confirmed in controlled research at several centers around the world. The use of these procedures, precisely and in a controlled situation, could bring a patient into a state of processing memories. The study also showed that negative thoughts and emotions tended to disappear when a patient used EMDR.

The EMDR approach gives us a model that enables us to understand how positive experiences support adaptive living and psychological health. It shows how experiences can sometimes lead to psychological problems that interfere with a person's ability to cope with life. The EMDR protocol guides therapists in careful assessment and preparation work, especially for those with histories of multiple traumas. A fully trained EMDR technician should, however, only use EMDR procedures.

Imagery

The gentle techniques of guided imagery can help us feel calm, and it grounds us in a safe place and gives us a sense of peace. Using guided imagery can help us to discover hidden resources that we didn't know that we had and to deal with overwhelming feelings. Imagery re-scripting uses the power of imagination and visualization to identify and change traumatic experiences that took place in the past. Imagery can result in the transformation of information from the past into the present.

The imagery process has five main components:

- A Client can process those emotions which are difficult to access.

- Care and support are provided, which would have been blocked during childhood.

- Issues that have influenced how a client feels about themselves can be externally reattributed, so transferring the blame from the child to someone else.

- The pain and trauma experienced due to the abuse are brought down to a "child level" or not rational or logical, but meaningful.

- The client begins to understand that the environment in which he or she grew up was an exception and not the norm.

Using imagery, a client is allowed to change the meaning of traumatic memories through unconditioned stimuli revaluation. New information is made available to the client who now has his or her needs met by fantasy. This can result in a change of meaning being attributed to traumatic memory. Techniques are not based on systematic desensitization principles, and therapists do not need to bring up the entire traumatic event.

When using the imagery process, it can be challenging for the client to recall specific traumatic events during childhood. The therapist takes the client through a journey of past events and memories, which may have contributed toward the trauma—for example, those feelings which are associated with feeling guilty or inadequate. The process leads the client into finding earlier images and bringing them forward so that they can be changed. If the therapist feels that the client is unable to provide the corrective emotional experience, fantasy, and positive visual images are then introduced.

Fantasy and visual images are limitless, so there is always something to help with a successful rescript. Therapists do, however, need to be tuned into the client to determine if this type of intervention is meaningful and helpful. The client needs to know that they are safe and that they can construct an image which allows for their safety.

Writing

Researching for as well as writing this book was a great healing process for me. So often, when we are abused as a child, no one will listen to us. Our experiences will be distorted, trivialized, or "swept under the carpet." Writing can be cathartic in getting our thoughts into the open. It is an invaluable tool for healing. Writing gives us the chance to be heard. We can write down our thoughts and let those who read our story realize that it wasn't our fault. That we were, and still are, innocent.

Sitting down and writing about what happened also allows us to experience feelings again, and we can grieve. We can rid ourselves of the sites where we buried these memories and to relive our trauma with the compassion and support of our adult self. Writing as a healing tool can be used anywhere. All you have to do is to sit down and write.

Psychedelic Therapy

It's interesting to note that psychedelics can also change how we look at the world in a healing way. Clinical studies have found that psychedelic experiences combined with psychotherapy can reverse treatment-resistant-depression and trauma by removing the sting from our traumatic memories. Those who have used psychedelics to heal have rated the experience as one of the five most meaningful treatments of their lives. The use of psychedelics remains illegal and should only be used in conjunction with licensed therapy, only if this is legally permitted.

Most people believe that psychedelics only have a use as illicit drugs and belong to the 1960s' era of free-spirited optimism. When writing this book, psychedelics include LSD, psilocybin, magic mushrooms and ecstasy or MDMA, and peyote. All of which are regarded as Schedule I substances by the government and have little medical value. Perhaps it's wrong to carry on thinking that these psychedelics should be locked up in guarded safes when they are making a comeback as part of psychiatric research?

One study revealed that after three doses of MDMA, administered under a psychiatrist's guidance, patients reported a fifty-six percent decrease on average, in the severity of their symptoms. By the end of the study, two-thirds of the participants no longer met the criteria for having PTSD. Follow up examinations found that improvements lasted for more than a year after the therapy. It is interesting to note that psychedelics are now considered to be an untapped resource in the treatment of trauma, abuse, and other mental issues.

System Desensitization

System desensitization depends on classical conditions. It is used to treat phobias. We are taught to replace a fear response to a phobia with a relaxation response. Relaxation and breathing techniques are taught first. When these have been mastered, a therapist will slowly introduce phobias or fears. System desensitization is usually only used by therapists who have practiced trauma rehabilitation for many years.

Behavior Therapy

Behavior therapy is a broad term that refers to clinical psychotherapy that uses techniques derived from behaviorism. It is the theory that animal and human behavior can be explained in terms of conditions. To understand their patients, therapists who practice behavior therapy look at all the learned behavior and how the environment may have affected this. Behavior therapy seeks to identify and change potentially self-destructive or unhealthy behaviors. The premise of this therapy is the idea that all actions are learned. If you have learned unhealthy behaviors, you can theoretically change them. This therapy focuses on current problems and how to change our behaviors.

Aversion therapy

Aversion therapy is used to treat problems like substance abuse and alcoholism. It teaches people to relate unpleasant stimuli to something undesirable. Usually, the unpleasant stimulus is something that causes discomfort. In aversion therapy, the therapist may teach us how to associate alcohol, smoking, and drug usage with an unpleasant memory.

Cognitive Behavioral Therapy

Cognitive Behavioral Therapy or CBT is an extremely popular therapy and one which has assisted me with my healing. I also went on to study this further during my training to be a counselor. CBT combines behavioral therapy with cognitive therapy. Treatment is centered around how someone's thoughts and beliefs influence their actions and moods. The focus is to take the patient's current problems and run through methods to solve them. The long-term goal with CBT is to change a person's negative thinking and behavioral patterns into thoughts and patterns that are healthy. CBT is usually a short-term and goal-oriented psychotherapy treatment that takes a hands-on, practical approach to problem-solving. The goal is to change the patterns of behavior or thinking that are the problems behind our difficulties.

The technique focuses on modifying dysfunction, emotions, behaviors, and thought by getting rid of irrational or negative beliefs, thoughts, and feelings. A solution-oriented form of talk therapy, CBT is based on the idea that our perceptions and thoughts influence our behavior. If we are distressed, that feeling can distort our perception of reality. CBT looks to identify harmful thoughts, assess whether they are accurate, and employ strategies to overcome trauma and difficulties.

This form of therapy is useful for people of all ages, including children. There is evidence of CBT addressing many conditions such as major depressive disorder, anxiety disorders, PTSD, obsessive-compulsive disorder, and eating disorders. It has become a preferred modality for therapists and insurance companies. CBT can help after five to twenty sessions, although there is no set time frame for this.

Cognitive Behavioral Play Therapy

Cognitive Behavioral Play Therapy or CBPT is often used with children. By watching a child play, therapists can gain an insight into what he or she is thinking, and what might be repressed. Children often play freely with their toys and watching this can give a therapist insight into what the child remembers of a memory that was buried. A frequently used technique in CBPT is to ask children to draw a picture or use their toys to create scenes. Children are innocent, so what they draw or build often represents the memories that they have buried. There has been a lot of progress in helping children heal from sexual abuse trauma because of CBPT. The therapist can see what the child feels, and healing can begin with talking and reforming their memories.

Hypnotherapy

Hypnotherapy is useful in helping us to cope with pain, stress, anxiety, and trauma. It is important to note that Cognitive Behavioral Therapy is considered being the first line of treatment for these conditions since it can be challenging to enter into a hypnotic state completely. Any traumatic event can cause us to disconnect from our sense of safety, which is required when entering into a hypnotic or a deep trance state. Hypnotherapy can help us to cope with trauma and allow us to learn how to regain control of our lives.

It aims to access our unconscious mind and change the negative thoughts that are holding us back. By using the power of suggestion, hypnotherapy can promote positive change. The recommendations used will depend on the symptoms and what clients want to change. Hypnotherapists usually tailor their techniques to help us as individuals to manage our symptoms, recognize the potential triggers, and then help us to improve how we react to them.

Using hypnotherapy can help us to become more receptive to suggestions and more able to change certain behaviors. It can also help change perceptions and sensations—especially when treating painful memories.

What is Hypnosis?

Hypnosis usually involves a person experiencing deep relaxation with their attention narrowed down and focused on appropriate suggestions for change and is generally facilitated by a hypnotist. During the hypnosis, breathing becomes slower and deeper, and pulse and metabolic rates drop. Similar changes occur in nervous pathways and hormonal systems, reducing the feelings of pain and anxiety and overcoming bad symptoms like nausea or indigestion.

Hypnosis is a common state of mind which everyone experiences at some stage in their life; here are some examples:

- While driving a vehicle, if you have missed your turn because you were contemplating a specific thought, this is an example of 'road-hypnosis.'

- When you reach your destination without even actively thinking about the journey, perhaps you were over-occupied by thoughts about something else; this is hypnosis.

- If you are watching television or reading a book and someone is talking to you, but you haven't heard a word that they say, you were experiencing a state of hypnosis.

Many people consider hypnosis as a state of a deep sleep, but in reality, it is a different state of mind. It is like a trance-like situation, but when in it, the person experiencing this feels more mindful and can concentrate on the hypnotist's voice. It suppresses the conscious mind and empowers the subconscious mind. When in the hypnotic state, the person is in a better position to accept ideas, beliefs, and lifestyle changes suggested by a therapist.

Hypnotherapy empowers individuals to make the right decisions and to bring constructive changes into their lives. Hypnotherapy is a type of psychotherapy that promotes positive development and healing processes. It is meant to reprogram the thinking behavior of the mind, enabling the person to get rid of illogical anxieties, phobias, pessimistic thoughts, and repressed emotions.

How does it work?

Hypnosis changes our state of consciousness by turning off the analytical left side of our brain and making the non-analytical right side of the brain more alert. It prohibits the conscious control of the mind and awakens the subconscious mind, bringing about long-lasting positive changes in behavior and the physical state.

For instance, a person who intentionally wants to get rid of fear related to a particular situation may do everything possible but fail to achieve the objective, unless their subconscious mind retains the anxiety associated with the situation. Betterment in such cases is only possible by reprogramming the subconscious mind so that the deep-rooted fears and negative thoughts can be discarded or changed.

Parts of the Human Mind

Conscious Mind

The Conscious Mind has four parts – rational, analytical, willpower, and temporary memory.

Though the conscious mind is the weakest part of our brain, we spend most of our time under its control. It is the logical and analytical part of the reason designed to think and judge different situations.

Our ability to rationalize is what makes humans unique, and this ability keeps us sane. Rational thinking may not be correct in all situations; for example, a victim of abuse may rationalize the abuse by saying, "It was my fault," but in reality, it is never the fault of the victim, but the responsibility of the abuser. The rational parts of our mind come up with some reasoning to keep us satisfied. The analytical mind identifies the issues and suggests ways to overcome them.

Willpower belongs to our conscious mind. You must have tried using willpower to get rid of an old habit, but willpower only has momentary effects. Willpower provides us with instant bursts of energy to help in a particular situation, but then it goes away, and we are back to the initial state of mind. Willpower can't bring permanent internal changes. The change will be permanent once our deeper or subconscious mind triggers it.

The fourth part of our conscious mind is our 'temporary memory,' which is very limited. It is the memory we all need to perform daily life activities such as memorizing our home address and our friends' names, etc. Scientific studies have shown that our conscious mind can hold a minimal amount of information at one time, and so is much weaker than our subconscious mind.

Subconscious Mind

The Subconscious Mind is the most influential part of our mind. It controls and assists you in achieving your objectives. It is the part of the brain that functions the most during hypnosis and the part that is related to all of our imaginations. Imaginations give an insight into our perception of the world, and naturally, everyone has a different perception. Perception is a kind of personal truth that a person believes and may not be the actual reality.

Our permanent memory is also associated with our subconscious mind. The input we receive from our five senses is permanently stored in our subconscious mind. Every event that occurred in our life left an impression on us. Based on the information, we develop our opinions and behaviors that, in turn, defines our personality. We think, act, and feel about every event that occurs in our lives in light of the long-term memories which are stored in the subconscious mind.

Our permanent memory is like a computer's hard disk, it is a very organized structure of information, and it works by association. For example, while you are driving a car hearing an old song, feelings associated with the music may come back to you, and you may start to think about some associated memory or person linked to that memory.

As we sometimes need to reprogram our computers, the same is the case with our subconscious mind, as this also requires reprogramming.

Behaviors, emotions, and opinions also reside inside the subconscious mind. Hypnosis helps you to become aware of your thoughts or feelings that are associated with your problems. When you let this happen, you embark on a journey that ends in a permanently changed state.

Our Autonomic Nervous System is programmed to function without requiring conscious thinking. These processes include breathing, eating, heart beating, and blood circulation, which are all activities that we perform without even giving them a thought. Our subconscious mind signals us in various situations. It takes appropriate decisions accordingly, such as when we are tired or hungry or injured in an accident.

Hypnotherapists use many techniques during the session, including 'inductions,' and these can have slow or fast outcomes, and they can be applied directly or indirectly. Once the patient enters into a hypnotic state, the therapist uses a 'deepener' which assists in intensifying the state of hypnosis, allowing the patient to settle and to become familiarized with the process.

Hypnotic Suggestions

Throughout the hypnotherapy process, the hypnotherapist often uses direct or indirect suggestions to induce change.

Direct suggestions are more authoritative and unequivocal, such as "let go of that tension… now…" These types of recommendations are appropriate for people who like a direct approach. Indirect language can also be used when a softer expression is required, such as "I wonder whether your left shoulder is relaxing now… or would you like to think about…"

Indirect hypnotherapy suggestions are useful when the client prefers to be part of a collaborative process or if the client doesn't like to be instructed to do something. Many therapists would employ both direct and indirect suggestion techniques during their sessions. The primary factor that helps during this decision is analyzing the client's 'locus of control.'

'Locus of control' is a psychological concept that is about a personality feature defined on a scale and states to which extent a person believes they have control over their life. The scale may have values like 'internal,' 'balanced,' and 'external.'

A person who has the value 'external' thinks that they are controlled by their fate and feel that they have little or no control over their life. Such a person does not take responsibility for their health or wellbeing. On the other hand, a person who is very 'internal' firmly believes that the duties of events are on their side. Still, in reality, some of those events are totally outside of their control.

For a balanced therapy session, it is beneficial if the client's locus of control is more 'balanced' rather than 'internal' or 'external' because such a person accepts appropriate responsibility for the process and has a positive interaction with the therapist. 'Locus of control' can be managed using 'ego-strengthening.'

Ego-strengthening enhances and balances the client's 'locus of control.' It also has positive benefits for self-esteem, confidence, and a sense of self. It empowers clients and enhances their resilience. It facilitates therapeutic processes that can bring about more effective and permanent positive changes. Ego-strengthening strategies can be either direct or metaphorical.

Metaphors

'Metaphorical' techniques are one of the aspects of the 'Ericksonian Hypnotherapy' method, which is considered extremely effective. We use metaphors in our spoken languages, such as 'her memory of the event was foggy' or 'All the world's a stage.' We are also acquainted with metaphorical stories. As a child, we were told stories, and those stories had a long-lasting impression on our thoughts, even without our consent.

To summarize, hypnotherapy affects each client and their issues differently. So, a hypnotherapy approach might require a single session or several sessions to obtain the desired results. Furthermore, as the therapy process is carried out, more issues may arise, which the client may not have been consciously mindful of. This is why a professional hypnotherapist would evaluate the client's overall objectives and establish goals for that session at the very beginning of the session.

Exposure Therapy

Exposure therapy is a psychological treatment developed to give people a way to confront their fears. When we are afraid of something, we tend to avoid the objective, activity, or situation. This avoidance can help reduce feelings of anxiety in the short term, but over the long term, it can make the fear worse. Psychologists can create a safe environment in which individuals can be exposed to the feelings that they fear and avoid. This exposure would then help to reduce this fear and decrease avoidance.

Exposure therapy helps treat phobias, panic disorders, social anxiety disorders, obsessive-compulsive disorder, PTSD, and generalized anxiety disorders.

Neurofeedback

Neurofeedback or EEG Biofeedback is based on electrical brain activity and uses an electroencephalogram or EEG to measure and learn about our brain functions. It is an efficient way to face trauma and learn more about how the brain and emotions change our brain waves. It can be an alternative form of treatment for childhood abuse, complex trauma, and PTSD.

Neurofeedback supplies information to the brain, which regulates the body's autonomic stress response. When we suffer from multiple traumatic events, including sexual abuse, violence, or even abandonment, this can result in us living in a perpetual state of sympathetic arousal or a parasympathetic response or shutdown.

Complex trauma may also have come from emotional abuse or neglect.

Neurofeedback uses a real-time display of brain activity in an attempt to teach self-regulation. Sensors are placed onto the scalp to measure electrical activity, and these measurements are displayed via video or sound. This treatment is not widely accepted in the mainstream therapy or medical community, and its validity has been questioned. However, it is still used as a complementary and alternative treatment for many brain dysfunctions, including trauma.

Group Therapy

Group therapy is highly effective for trauma victims. It strengthens relationship skills, reduces isolation, and helps us to find our voice. Taking part in group therapy, we quickly realize that we are not alone. It is true that everyone is unique and has different circumstances, but we are not alone in our struggles. In a group session detailed in The Theory and Practice of Group Psychotherapy by Irvin D Yalom, many patients didn't believe that they could ever talk about their trauma or distress. They were sufferers of terrible problems, thoughts, and impulses. Upon discussions, it was discovered in the group therapy session that nearly everyone felt alienated and was worried that they wouldn't be able to care for or to love someone else. It was also found that most of the group had a sexual abuse secret, making them feel inadequate and incompetent.

Group therapy helps us find our voice. To become aware of our feelings and needs, and to learn how to express them so that we can connect to others and, in turn, listen to their issues. We may be able to relate to others and ourselves in healthier ways. Group therapy provides us with a safety net as we know that we have the group's support, and we can carry this knowledge with us between sessions. It makes it easier to take risks if we know that we have others who care about us and who will listen to our experiences and that there will be someone to catch us if we fall.

Acupuncture for Treating Trauma

Pilot studies have shown that acupuncture can help those with PTSD. Seventy-three people who had PTSD took part in a study in which they received either acupuncture or group Cognitive Behavioral Therapy (CBT) over twelve weeks. It was only a small group, but the results instigated other studies using acupuncture as a treatment. Researchers found that it gave similar results to group CBT. The effects of acupuncture and group therapy lasted for three months after the study ended, with excellent results for acupuncture.

The Essential Breath

Did you know that breathing deeply and correctly through our nostrils rather than our mouths, can help us to heal?

To give ourselves instantaneous and youthful energy, we often turn to synthetic uppers like alcohol and drugs or maybe even large doses of vitamins and herbs. We also turn to tranquilizers and sleeping pills to silence the sound in our minds. At other times, we may exist on the excitement of using sex or an obsession with work and material possessions to ignite our lives. All the while, knowing that there is something more, but not what that is.

Breathing is the most accessible resource we have for sustaining our energy. Tapping into this resource involves unleashing the essential breath. Most of us who have undergone trauma, and lost connection with our inner self, need to get back to this crucial breath, a natural energy resource. Once we open the door to the right way to breathe, we can rediscover energy sources we never knew that we had. I learned about the importance of breathing through yoga and meditation.

Anu Verma

Chapter VI: Treatment for Child and Adult Abuse

Physical abuse of a child often leads to physical and mental difficulties in the future. Re-victimization; personality disorder; PTSD; dissociative disorders; depression; anxiety or suicidal ideation; eating disorders; substance abuse; and aggressive tendencies are only a few of the things a child will suffer from when abused. They will often have difficulties with interpersonal relationships, especially trust, compared to those who have not been abused.

The betrayal of trust and violation of personal boundaries involved in child sexual abuse brings a sense of shame, guilt, and confusion. This disrupts the child's internal working model. Sexual abuse changes how a child interprets the world and changes how a child. Then, as an adult, it impacts how one understands and looks at the motives and behaviors of others. It changes how he or she handles stressful life events.

There is evidence of adults, who were sexually abused as children, and who were experiencing more significant difficulties in interpersonal and intimate relationships. Increased instability in those relationships, more sexual partners, and an increased risk of sexual problems and negativity toward partners are evident. I suffered from mistrust, difficulties in interpersonal and intimate relationships.
I distrusted men to the point where I wouldn't believe what they said. I became almost manic in my sexual activity. I didn't enjoy intimacy, and I thought of sex as "a game." Reflecting, I had many

destructive partners who were reaching out for me to heal them while I couldn't help them because I couldn't even help myself!

The Later Consequences of Abuse

A child may have witnessed their parents' abusive relationship and had grown up with the belief that this was normal. It is essential to encourage the child and to plant the seed that they can look at relationships differently. Ask them to write down what he or she thinks having a healthy relationship will involve. Talk about what is expected and what isn't. Reassure them that the pattern of abuse witnessed as a child doesn't need to carry on into the present or the future.

It is a recognized statistic that many people who were abused as children grow up to become adults who abuse. A therapist can present strategies to help abused clients replace their current feelings about the abuse. They can teach coping skills that will help them to calm down, to work through their anger, anxiety, or depression in a positive and non-abusive manner, avoid making assumptions. Men abusing women does happen in the majority of cases, but abuse can occur in all types of situations. There is an added danger in abusive relationships that involve people with disabilities, same-sex couples, and members of minority cultures.

It's vital to factor in trauma when discussing the abuse with a client. So much so that it becomes unethical and inaccurate to diagnose anyone without journaling his or her abuse history. It is impossible to work through a client's problems without any regard for what trauma and abuse can do to someone's life.

Treatment for Child Abuse

Treatment is essential to help children and parents or caregivers in abusive situations. The priority is to find safety for the children who are being or have been abused. Ongoing treatment means preventing future abuse and reducing the long term psychological and physical consequences of this.

Psychotherapy is essential in the healing processes used for abused children. Talking with a therapist can help a child in learning to trust. To teach him or her about normal behaviors, to learn conflict management, and to boost self-esteem. It may, however, take a lot of therapy and a very long time for a child to heal and to be able to trust.
Different types of therapy that may be helpful in abusive situations include:

Trauma-focused Cognitive Behaviors Therapy

CBT helps children to reframe how they evaluate their emotional and behavioral reactions to negative experiences. CBT teaches children that their thoughts can influence their emotions, and their behavior is essential. Knowing that emotions and behavior can be assessed and managed is empowering. It leads to an improvement in self-control, emotions, coping skills, and reactions to negative experiences. CBT advances recovery by encouraging children to open up and to talk freely about their trauma. Trauma-focused CBT promotes the importance of walking through the trauma, using gradual exposure as a means for the child to come to terms with what happened. It stresses moving on and letting go of the trauma.

Anxiety disorders are a form of psychopathology in children and adolescents. Symptoms of Generalized Anxiety Disorder (GAD) in children are often exhibited as being almost obsessed with their health, what is happening at school, the health of loved ones, opinions of others, and social issues. Therapists are cautious when using CBT with an abused child. There are potential adverse outcomes that, when coupled with the child's immature mind, can be detrimental in several ways.

Numerous clinical trials have established the effectiveness of CBT as a means of treating children with anxiety disorders. In 2003, Reinecke, Dattilio & Freeman found that between fifty-five and sixty-five percent of children who underwent CBT almost completely recovered from an anxiety disorder. The results of this particular study also indicate that CBT is potentially valuable in assisting very young children (under the age of seven years) in managing moderate anxiety from abuse.

Beck (1979) suggested that individuals have particular thoughts and related behaviors when they are in a depressed mood. People who are depressed tend to focus on the bad things that have happened to them while often overlooking the good in their lives. Studies indicate that thirty to forty percent of adolescents will experience an episode of major depressive disorder. The most influential risk factors include genetic susceptibility to depression, following exposure to psychosocial stress, such as parental divorce, domestic violence, and abuse.

One of the most toxic but common results of trauma resulting from sexual abuse is for children to think that it was their fault, or something is wrong with them. They may feel like they did something which resulted in the situation that occurred. This is why being open and communicative about their feelings, and to gradually expose the trauma, can be beneficial in helping them to overcome these feelings.

In summary, CBT's goal is to identify negative thoughts and replace them with positive ones. Change can be accomplished by using positive behavioral skills to attain positive moods and healthy relationships.

Child-Parent Psychotherapy

Child-parent psychotherapy is a relationship-based treatment for young children and their parents. It aims to help restore normal developmental functions after domestic violence, trauma, and sexual abuse. Child-parent psychotherapy is based on attachment theory, but it also integrates social learning, developmental psychodynamic trauma, social learning, and cognitive-behavioral approaches. Sessions involve the parent or primary caregiver, plus the child. The primary goal of therapy is to support and to strengthen relationships between a child and his or her caregiver. It is a way of restoring a child's cognitive, social, and behavioral functioning.

Coping and Support

As a sexual abuse survivor, I understand the importance of opening up to an adult about what happened. The child can only open up to an adult if they feel like they can trust them and to have somebody who would believe them. Children aren't naturally taletellers so more than likely; if they mention that they are being abused, they must surely be. If this is the case, then it is essential to take the following actions:

- Encourage the child to explain what has occurred. Stay relaxed while reminding the child that the incident is okay to discuss. Let the child believe that the best choice they have right now is to talk, even if they have been threatened by the abuser to remain quiet. Concentrate on listening. Do not ask a lot of questions or for detailed information.

- Try to convince the child that the abuse is not his or her fault. The child wants to be assured that this is not their fault.

- Give reassurance. You might say, "I'm very sorry that you've been hurt" or "I'm happy that you've told me." Let the child know that you're around to talk to and to listen.

- Report the harassment. Call your local child protection service or the police. These officials are allowed to ascertain the report. Take some action, if needed, to ensure the safety of the child.

- Make the child feel secure and safe. Separate and protect the child from the abuser.

- Seek medical help so that a full examination can be carried out. Seek some form of therapy for mental wellbeing. Perhaps same-age support groups could also help.

- If the abuse occurred at school, inform the school headteacher. Ensure that the officials are notified of the incident. Remove the child from the school, if required.

Therapy for Adult Abuse

It is documented that more than one-third of women and a quarter of men have experienced rape, physical abuse, or stalking. These statistics alone suggest that counselors and therapists, from school counselors to addiction counselors, are likely to encounter clients who have been abused.

Physical abuse often results in the victim suffering from anxiety and issues with his or her self-esteem. There is also a wide range of other symptoms, from relationship challenges to financial and employment problems. One of the most prevalent abuse patterns, in addition to child abuse, is domestic violence.

When working with adult abuse in a therapy situation, the first consideration is the client's safety and well-being. Simply asking if they need help can put the abused adult in danger, should the abuser become aware that they are seeking therapy. If the abused adult is more assertive when he or she returns home, this may lead to further abuse.

A safety plan should be created. Intervention can be done with children and adults to keep them safe. One idea might be holding an extra house key and changing clothes in a car if the abused person is thrown out of their house.

The majority of therapists agree that they need to step outside the counseling box and work with other agencies in the community. These include abuse hotlines, shelters, school resource officers, women's clinics, victim advocate organizations, and support groups. Law enforcement personnel and social workers, who have experience with victims of abuse, also work alongside therapists.

Victims of abuse also require social support. Sufferers of trauma need to learn how to rebuild relationships with friends and family, who may have been cut off from the victim's life while the abuse was taking place. When talking with survivors, counselors and therapists have found that they crave the opportunity to tell their story to a trusted helper. Talking this through counseling sessions gives survivors the power to heal and to help him or her to feel validated.

Journaling is also a useful therapy tool. Writing down their traumatic experiences can help survivors of abuse. They can learn coping techniques, how to deal with stress, set goals, relax, and to write down their stories in such a way that they provide self-reflection and self-care. Each of these techniques is about helping survivors to recreate their own identity on their terms.

Part III: Healing and Victory

Chapter I: Traveling

How Traveling Helped me to Heal

I have always enjoyed traveling and the exposure it gave me to different cultures and experiences. I learned so much from it. Most importantly, I realized how much better it is to look at other people and places with an 'open mind.' I used to travel in the past as a form of escapism and not realizing the therapeutic benefit which I was experiencing because of it. Traveling was a form of healing for me.

Traveling and exploring different places has enormous benefits. It's lovely to meet new people and to hear their unique stories. I gained a much better understanding of the culture and history of the places I visited by talking to and seeing the local population.

I would like to share with you the great benefits of traveling as it can not only improve our overall health, but it may also boost our creative skills. The benefits of traveling include the following:

- **It helps us to be Grateful** - It's often said that we never know what we have until we lose it, and sadly there is truth in this statement. Traveling also gives us a break from a hectic daily routine and empowers us to be thankful for the people and things that we have in our life.

- **Enhances Creative Thoughts** - Creativity can be triggered when we are taken outside of our comfort zone. Traveling takes us away from our everyday life, the people we know, and the places. It causes us to experience different situations. This boosts our creative abilities and out of the box thinking.

- **Opens up our Mind** - Traveling allows us to learn about the challenges faced by people in other cultures, and it broadens our horizons.

- **Helps us to Cope** - As situations can unexpectedly change during traveling, this helps us learn to cope with uncertainty or the unusual, more patiently and calmly.

- **Gives us Courage** - Traveling allows us to become more confident by allowing us to interact independently with people whom we do not know and to cope with challenges in a new place.

- **Gives us Real Life Wisdom** - Although formal education is essential, traveling often provides us with a pearl of wisdom, otherwise impossible to attain.

- **Helps us to get to Know Ourselves** - Being in situations that often seem strange, when we travel, enables us to understand how to react to them and to be more prepared if something similar happens in the future.

Chapter II: Relationships

What I Learned from Relationships

I could certainly say that the thought of love blindsided me as I needed to be wanted by somebody. After all of my relationships, which did not work, I do not regret any of them. I have learned so much, and I have grown so much from all of my past experiences. These lessons do help us to have better relationships in the future.

Once the trauma and anger vanish, we can come out on the other side as a more positive person with a more profound outlook. Here are a few of the lessons that I have learned from the harsh experiences that I suffered from:

- **You are Priority** - Make yourself your number one priority. People may take advantage of you unfairly when you show unconditional courtesy.

- **Shared Values** - There must be a substantial number of shared values for a relationship to prosper. Ask yourself if you or your partner has significant differences in many respects. Are you willing to compromise and to change yourself for your partner's satisfaction?

- **Care and Compromise** - Care and compromise are good habits to have, and you deserve them from others too. Unilaterally compromising on others' mistakes can lead to them taking advantage of you.

- **Communication is Key** - Although it is usually considered that arguments are part of a relationship, it is much better to have a productive dialogue and be generous and respectful.

- **Believe in Each Other** - It is a huge blessing if your partner believes in your abilities and supports you even if you fail. Choosing a partner with these traits will give you feelings of trust and safety.

- **You Deserve to be Treated Well** - Don't let someone else make you feel bad about yourself and don't compromise on your self-respect. We all deserve to be loved and to be treated kindly.

- **Do Not Forget Your Family and Friends** - It is sometimes said that a person is known by the company they keep. Friends and family of your partner are often a true reflection of what kind of person they are.

- **Do Not 'Fake It Until You Make It'** - If you find that you cannot be yourself in front of your partner, this may not be the person for you. Your partner should accept your real self. Otherwise, the relationship is not worth maintaining.

Chapter III: Life Skills

Life Skills which I Learned to Improve Relationships

Though break-ups are disastrous, they also teach us valuable lessons, which can completely change our thoughts about relationships, even if it's that you never want to experience one again! By looking into the deepest part of ourselves, identifying any inner weaknesses, and reflecting on this, the end of a relationship moves us closer to the one we truly want.

Failed relationships teach us that we are capable of so much more. To feel fulfilled in ways that we have never experienced before. With so many relationships that never succeeded under my belt, I made it a priority to look deeper within and to understand what valuable lessons each one of the break-ups had taught me. Here are some key reminders that I live by:

- **Maintain Your Independent Self** - You should not completely lose your personality for the sake of a relationship. Developing boundaries are important while having activities and interests outside of the relationship is healthy. Talk through and create these boundaries early on, to avoid becoming co-dependent on each other. Breakups are not joyful events, but if you can learn from the mistakes that you made in your previous relationship, then you are heading in the right direction.

VICTIM 2 VICTOR

- **Live in The Present Moment** - The past is the past, and the future is the future, over which we don't have any control. Worrying about or manipulating your present moment will not change your future in any way. So, by not controlling the outcome of your relationship, you get to be more present.

- **Do Not Rush into a Relationship** - Rushing into a relationship is like fireworks, which quickly burn out. What is essential is to take things slowly because true love takes time to mature.

- **Be A Responsible Person** - Taking responsibility for your actions and not blaming others and admitting if you are wrong shows emotional maturity. This will help you in your future relationships. You can choose how you react to your partner, even though you cannot control what he or she says or does.

- **Past Relationships are There to Learn from** - It's very tempting to label failed relationships as a mistake, although a wrong decision hasn't been made. Don't be sad or have any regrets regarding your past experiences.

- **Your Needs Are Genuine** - You should not be ashamed of your genuine needs and realize that your feelings, perspectives, time, and preferences are all valid and valuable. So, in your relationship, you have a right to expect and to accept nothing less.

- **Small Things May Have a Huge Impact** - Signs of jealousy and control early in the relationship will only worsen if they are not dealt with. Even signs which may seem small at first can become huge later on.

- **Explore the Opportunities** - You can't change anybody, so never just settle for anybody. Instead, think about what you desire from your next relationship. How would you like your partner to interact with you? Will this partner meet your needs?

- **Style of Communication Can Change Anything** - People learn about themselves and their communication styles in failed relationships. It is wise to ask yourself how you responded to arguments. Did you become apologetic or critical? If so, you may need to work on communicating better with your new partner. The key to a healthy relationship is communication. To be able to identify destructive patterns and to replace them with healthier ways of communication will help to resolve conflict.

- **Retain Other Relationships -** It is crucial to sustaining other relationships in life that help with our development, to enable us to live fuller lives and to be better partners. It is up to us to keep ourselves happy and content, and we should not rely on our partner to keep us happy.

Chapter IV: Introduction to Energy Healing

I will now share my journey to victory, which I hope is of value to you too. I will discuss energy healing, various therapy modalities, as well as techniques that I used. This all played an essential part in helping me to overcome the hurt, pain, and sadness that was upon me as a result of the abuse and trauma that I had experienced throughout my life.

Energy healing is holistic and activates the body's energy systems to remove blocks that cause emotional or physical problems. Energy healing enables the body's energy systems to cure, and once the body has broken through these energy blocks, the body's ability to heal itself is stimulated. The body's energy is not a new concept; it has been studied for thousands of years. Ancient cultures use different ways to boost the body's natural energy to heal, and they all recognize the power of your internal energy.

Your body's energy is based upon scientific facts. The matter is made up of molecules, and everything stable vibrates all the time. When you talk about "good vibes," you are talking about a person's vibrational energy. It is a scientific fact that happy and energized people vibrate at a higher frequency.

It doesn't matter who you are or what you have been through; anyone benefits from energy healing. It is not necessary to understand the concept of energy feeling before you can benefit from it. Just remember that if you are stressed, anxious, or physically drained, energy healing sessions done in many different ways can help you to relax and to feel balanced.

Energy Healing Modalities

Different types of healing modalities are available. Each one has various tools and techniques, but each one will help you to remove the energy blocks that you are feeling.

- **Reiki** - A Japanese tradition of energy healing dates to the early 20th century and balances the seven chakras.

- **Yoga** - Stresses meditation, working with your body and breath, and finding your center of energy.

- **Acupuncture** - Small needles are used to stimulate the flow of energy in the body.

- **Reflexology** - A modality that frees up block energy and promotes healing by stimulating pressure points on your hands, ears, and feet.

- **Massage** - An energy healing practice designed to release tension in the muscles and to encourage the flow of lymph that clears the body of toxins, waste, and other unwanted materials.

- **Soaking** - Bathing with Epsom or pink Himalayan salts can help balance the body by removing harmful toxins from the body.

- **Smudging** -Burning sage around, you can help to clear the air, and it releases negative ions which are linked to positive moods

- **Crystals** - Using crystals can all help to cleanse the energy around you and rid of negative energy.

Chapter V: Reiki

As mentioned in an earlier section of this book, I studied Reiki to promote healing and change in my own life. The powers of Reiki energy allowed me to heal most blissfully. I was able to let go of my traumas and make room for peace and light to enter within me. The powers of Reiki also allowed me to pick up on energies very intuitively, and it gave me the gift of keeping negative energies and those people with unkind intentions at bay. This has led me to a more positive and successful journey, which has ultimately contributed toward my road to victory.

Reiki is a healing technique based on the theory that the master or therapist can channel energy into a patient or someone else by touch. Touch activates the natural healing processes of the receiver's body, and physical and emotional wellbeing is restored.

Reiki is amazingly simple to learn but is not a classroom curriculum and is not just "touch." Reiki is transferred to a student during a Reiki class. The Reiki Master passes on Reiki during an attunement given by the master. The master allows the student to find an unlimited supply of life force energy to improve health and enhance the quality of life.

Reiki is not dependent on your intellectual capacity or spiritual development and is available to everyone. Thousands of people of all ages and backgrounds have entered the healing energy of Reiki. Reiki is spiritual, but it is not a religion. It has no doctrine, and there is nothing you must believe in to learn and use Reiki. Reiki is not dependent on belief and will work whether you believe in it or not. Reiki comes from God and puts people in touch with the experiences of religion, life, and their past, present, and future.

Reiki is essential to living and acts in a way that promotes harmony with others. The Reiki system of natural healing, Mikao Usui, recommended that you practice certain simple ethical ideals to find peace and harmony. These noble ideas are universal across all cultures and religions.

The concept of Reiki comes in part from the five principles of the Meiji Emperor of Japan, who Mikao Usui admired. The ideals were formed to add spiritual balance to Usui Reiki. The purpose is to help you realize that healing the spirit, by consciously deciding to develop yourself, is an integral part of the Reiki healing experience.

Reiki healing energies will work if you accept responsibility for your healing and participate in it. You must have an active commitment to developing yourself and to use Reiki as a complete system. The ideals of Reiki are a guide for living a gracious life and following virtues worth of practice.

Reiki is an aid to relaxation and assists the body's natural healing processes. It induces deep relaxation, helps people cope with traumas and difficulties, relieves emotional stresses, and improves overall wellbeing. To put it simply, the spiritual healing art of Reiki works by channeling positive energy into your body. Reiki masters and practitioners place their hands on the area of the body that needs energy. The master offers energy, and your body takes in the energy where it is most needed.

Let's describe Reiki healing in another way. The spiritual healing of Reiki works by channeling positive energy into your body by a Reiki master or a practitioner. The powerful flow of positive energy may bring a near-immediate sensation of relief since it is designed to release tension, lessen the impact of stress, and replace negative energy. Positive Reiki energy is often referred to as the 'life force.' It can bring relief to a stressed out and tired body.

Reiki may potentially help you to enjoy and to understand that you do not need to have headaches, body aches, or angry outbursts. When you are less stressed, you can think with greater clarity. You are less likely to be consumed by fear. Think about when you felt the happiest. Just thinking about what you were doing when you were happy will help you pinpoint the type of environment that gives you happiness.

Reiki can clear out fears, assist with clarity of mind, and enhance spiritual development. It can give you the confidence and energy that you need to move forward in pursuing your passion or rebuilding your life. You know things are good when your life seems to fall naturally into place.

To summarize the benefits of Reiki healing:

- Promotes harmony and balance since Reiki is an effective and non-invasive energy healing modality. Reiki enhances the body's natural healing ability.

- It creates relaxation and helps your body to release stress and tension. Reiki allows you time to understand yourself and takes you to a feeling of "being."

- Dissolves energy blocks and brings on a calmer and more peaceful state of mind and being. Reiki gives you the tools to cope with stress.
- Promotes a natural balance between our mind, body, and spirit and stops spending so much time in the stress reactions or the flight or flight phase. It teaches our bodies how to return to balance.

- It assists our body in cleansing itself from toxins and supports the immune system.

- Clears your mind and improves your focus. We feel centered and grounded, and clarity of mind places us in the present rather than letting us get caught up in regrets about the past or anxieties about the future.

- Aids better sleep and helps you to relax. When we are relaxed, we sleep better, and our bodies can heal, our minds think more clearly, and we can relate to each other more gently.

- Accelerates the body's self-healing ability as you return to a natural state and improves your heart and blood pressure. As you breathe deep through Reiki, your mind naturally settles. It is scientifically supported that Reiki or mindfulness helps your body to heal.

- It helps to relieve pain and supports the physical body in healing. Hands-on reiki encourages your body's vital functions, like breathing, digesting, and sleeping. These essential functions keep your body functioning, and reiki can create subtle shifts from deep within your being.

- It provides spiritual growth and emotional cleansing. Guidance comes more quickly about what to do in uncomfortable situations. Reiki might inspire a change of attitude, and you see your condition from a fresh perspective.

- Compliments medical treatment. Reiki provides relaxation, and when you are relaxed, the healing process is accelerated. You find you are healing when you sleep when you are calm and relaxed.

Chapter VI: Yoga and Healing Powers

Yoga has helped me to heal from life's trauma and depression.

I gained my yoga teacher qualification to learn more about the various postures (asanas) and how they benefit the mind, body, and soul. Gaining this qualification meant that I could practice yoga and teach those around me the true benefits that this fantastic healing practice can have on all of us.

Statistics reveal that people around the world are practicing yoga in ever-increasing numbers. This is due to evidence showing that yoga therapy is one of the most effective complementary treatments for different diseases and common ailments, including anxiety, heart disease, hypertension, diabetes, and arthritis.

Mainstream medical practices, as well as corporate organizations, are also embracing yoga therapies. Research has proven yoga's efficacy in aiding recovery, particularly from stress-related conditions, and improving overall health and vitality. Statistics show that sixty to eighty percent of complaints from patients have been caused by stress, and yoga is effective in managing and preventing stress-induced illnesses.

Anu Verma

Practicing yoga brings on a substantial benefit to your physical health. Yoga can transform your body into a body that is stronger, leaner, and able to withstand illnesses and diseases.

Yoga also transforms your mind. Think of yoga as an exercise routine for your mind. When you exercise and cultivate your mind, you improve your physical health and mental strength, and you add years to your life.

Yoga is also a workout for our inner self. Condition your inner being like your muscles, to develop and to grow stronger mentally. Yoga clears your mind from distracting issues, and it creates space to help new thoughts, ideas, and goals to develop and to grow.

Yoga restores balance and self-worth. You are empowered, and you can discover yourself on a more intimate and soulful level. You can identify who you are, and it becomes easier for you to focus and be creative. Yoga can lead you down a path to new ideas, purposes, and solutions to your problems.

Yoga and Meditation

Trauma therapist Bessel van der Kolk, M.D., has researched yoga, and his studies show a significant decrease in trauma symptoms with consistent yoga practice. There is still a debate going on to determine if yoga truly helps trauma victims, but the results which are showing are promising.

In conjunction with yoga, meditation is a fantastic bio-hack. You can do it anywhere and at any time, and it does work for building a healthier brain and becoming more aware of your emotions.

Regularly meditating relieves chronic stress and boosts alpha brain waves. Meditation also increases emotional regulation, emotional intelligence, self-awareness, and creativity—all the things that trauma decreases.

VICTIM 2 VICTOR

As you increase your emotional self-awareness through meditation, it will become easier for you to uncover negative brain loops caused by trauma, see them for what they are, and rewire your responses.

Forgiveness is the quickest way to let go of painful experiences and to boost alpha waves permanently. Facing trauma, feeling the pain, finding forgiveness, and letting the trauma go with the guidance of a qualified therapist, rewires your brain. With neurofeedback, you can teach your mind to release trauma and to become stronger.

Yoga and Healing from Trauma

Yoga is not the first-line treatment for trauma. Yoga does not heal traumatic memories via memory reconsolidation or any other techniques that help provide trauma healing. Still, yoga does help in reducing and managing the symptoms.

Trauma affects the brains of people who have experienced it, and it prevents your body from obtaining clear information from your mind. It has been shown that dysregulated body experiences hinder a person's ability to regulate their emotional or physical responses to the world. Trauma survivors experience hyperarousal, avoidance, and re-experiencing symptoms or flashbacks and intrusive thoughts.

Yoga has had a profound effect during my healing, and it has made me feel more present and grounded. I am more aware of what is going on around me when my mind draws me back to reliving my traumas from the past. Yoga helps bring me back to the present as it has the beautiful magic of connecting the body to the mind. Yoga has taken away the stress and has shown me more to life than my trauma.

Flashbacks to previous traumatic events can be triggered by anything that remotely resembled the trauma. Television programs, people arguing on the street, or pushing and shoving each other, can all be triggers. Reliving painful events is a common symptom of PTSD or chronic anxiety disorder that develops after being involved in a traumatic event. The traumatic events include sexual or physical abuse, war, natural disaster, or even car accidents. Existing treatments like therapy and drugs, only go so far. Yoga can complement any ongoing medical and mental procedures.

Yoga is excellent in easing the mind when flashbacks or feelings of past abuse creep up. In a study published in the Annuals of the New York Academy of Sciences, a PTSD expert discovered that a group of patients who took part in Hatha yoga classes showed improvements in their recovery symptoms from PTSD. The frequency of intrusive thoughts, depression, and stress was eased as this group of patients worked through yoga poses (asanas).

Yoga is a safe and gentle way of becoming acquainted with your body. You notice how things function inside your own body. Relaxation and breathing techniques help PTSD patients to calm themselves when they sense a flashback or a panic attack. Yoga emphasizes self-acceptance that is important for the victim of sexual assault.

Bessel van der Kolk, a professor of psychiatry at the Boston University School of Medicine and director of the Trauma Center, has studied trauma since the 1970s. He is a pioneer in the field of treating and describing trauma. Van der Kolk discovered that therapists who treated psychological trauma needed to work with the body and the mind. Hatha yoga became van der Kolk's yoga of choice, and he quickly became convinced that Hatha yoga could help his patients.

The U.S. military has investigated yoga's therapeutic potential. In a preliminary study at Walter Reed Army Medical Center in Washington, C.D., many active-duty soldiers who had PTSD were feeling less depressed after twelve weeks of Yoga Nidra or yogic sleep. The relaxation techniques which they learned helped them to feel more comfortable with situations that seemed out of control. As a result, these soldiers felt more in control over their lives.

An interesting fact about yoga for PTSD or trauma healing is that some trauma survivors found yoga threatening first. It proved to be more than many traumatized women could handle. You need to work at discovering your body and learning to be at one with your body when you engage in yoga practice. To these women, it was easier just to take a painkiller or an antidepressant pill to ease their symptoms.

In one yoga class, a woman who was participating found that the Happy Baby pose was just too emotional. In the Happy Baby pose, you lie on your back, bend your knees, with your lower legs perpendicular to the floor, and you hold your feet. Another participant who suffered from sexual abuse in early childhood disliked the Happy Baby pose. She felt that this pose was a baby waiting to be hurt.

Yoga masters taught the pose with an emphasis on comfort. If the pose and the name made patients uncomfortable, they were encouraged to work through their feelings. Those who stuck with the pose made extraordinary changes. Those who could not tolerate the Happy Baby pose were encouraged to try other gentle and comforting poses like the Child's Pose.

One student, after weeks of trying, now relaxes calmly into the Happy Baby pose. She says that yoga's effect has been exciting. It has taught her that she can overcome trauma and pain. After more than twenty years of therapy, she could function without self-destructive behaviors, and yoga gave her peace of mind.

Bessel van der Kolk illustrates a yoga model designed for survivors of complex interpretational trauma. His model shows increased activity in the interoceptive region of your brain, resulting in decreased PTSD symptoms. The model gives participants knowledge and feeling in their bodies when they extend their muscles in yoga practices. This flexing and stretching of muscles rebuild or rewire interoceptive regions of the brain. This research developed trauma-sensitive yoga. Trauma-sensitive yoga is very gentle. It is designed to build up the parasympathetic nervous system and encourages rest and digest instead of fight or flight.

Anu Verma

Trauma healing using yoga helps you be a more powerful person.

Yoga Poses for Healing Traumatic Experiences

Here are some great poses to try, which may help you to ease your trauma:

- **Child's Pose** - Sit on your heels and bring your head down to the floor. Bring your big toes to touch, knees the width of your mat, and reach your arms away from your body. Sit your hips back toward your heels and let your forehead come to the mat. Inhale into space between your ribs and your lower back. On each exhalation, allow your belly and chest to drop closer to the mat. Child's Pose is resting and will bring your body back to the present moment, give you the tools for meditation, and help you relax.

- **Extended Puppy Pose** - From a tabletop position, walk your hands away from your body and keep your hips stacked over your knees. Bring your forehead (or the chin) to the mat. Keep your arms to your side by pressing your forearms and hands down. On an inhalation, expand into your back body; on an exhalation, allow your heart to settle toward the floor. This pose opens up tension in your shoulders.

- **Downward-Facing Dog** - Keep a soft bend in your knees to encourage your tailbone to point up toward the ceiling, elongating the spine. Press the space between your shoulder blades up toward the ceiling, and press down into your hands, knuckles, and fingertips. Keep your neck neutral while your eyes look to the middle of your mat. When you inhale, press the ground away from you, and on exhaling, move your heels to come closer to the floor. This pose helps you slow your breath and rest. I practice downward facing dog every morning and maintain this posture for ten breaths, which helps to ground me and to set me up for the day.

- **Chair Pose** - Shift the weight in your feet toward your heels and keep your knees stacked over your ankles as you sit back. Hug your belly toward your spine and encourage your tailbone to reach down toward the ground. Draw your lower ribs in toward the stomach to activate your core. Reach your fingertips up toward the ceiling and rotate your pinky fingers in so your biceps frame your ears. Inhale and reach your fingertips away from your shoulders. When you exhale, sit back and down a little deeper—a pose for strengthening the body and the mind.

- **Warrior II** - From a wide-legged stance, place your front foot, so it faces forward, with your front knee stacked over your ankle and in line with your second and third toes. Rotate your back foot slightly. Your foot, knee, and hip should be in the same line. Anchor your weight into both feet evenly and draw your belly button up and back toward the spine. Stretch your arms away from your body to a T-shape and focus your eyes across the top of your hand. On each inhalation, reach your arms farther away from each other; on your exhalations, bend a little more into the front knee. This is a challenging pose that keeps your mind and body occupied.

- **Eagle Pose** - Root through all four corners of your right foot. Wrap your left leg over your right leg, and then wrap your left foot around your right ankle. Squeeze your thighs together and draw your belly button up and back toward the spine. Wrap your left arm under the right and bring your palms (or back of your hands) to touch. Reach your fingertips toward the ceiling and feel your shoulder blades glide down your back. On the inhalation, squeeze your thighs and arms together; on each exhalation, sit a little bit deeper. Then, repeat on your opposite leg. This pose will keep you in the present instead of letting your mind wander back to traumatic events.

- **Constructive Rest** - Lie flat on your back; knees bent, soles of your feet on the outer edges of your mat. Knock your knees in toward each other to release your lower back. Relax your neck and shoulders and bring one hand to your heart and the other to your belly. Close your eyes. On each inhalation, feel your hands rise as you expand your front body and chest. On each exhalation, allow your body to be heavy. This yoga pose brings awareness to your physical space and body.

As you work through yoga poses, you steadily become empowered to discover yourself. You can focus on and become creative. Stress works itself out of your body. Stress is a 'silent killer,' and yoga is the 'ultimate stress reducer.' When you breathe in deeply, focus on your poses. You will reduce anxiety, and you enter a relaxed state. Your nervous system is calmed, and the fight-or-flight response is diminished.

Anu Verma

Kundalini Yoga is another form of yoga that has helped me to heal and one which had left me so intrigued that I decided to study it further to understand the history of Kundalini and why it is such a powerful ancient practice.

Kundalini focuses on intense awareness and transformation. It stimulates powerful energy in your body, and it can renovate your life.

Experienced yoga instructors appreciate all kinds of yoga, including Hatha; Ashtanga; Bikram; Iyengar; Yoga Nidra, and Yin Yoga. But when super magical positive impacts are required, to shatter fear and your limiting beliefs. Kundalini Yoga is one of the popular choices.

Kundalini Yoga has several benefits, some of which are listed below:

- **Opens Up Your Energy Field** - By using sound, mantra, energy healing, exercises, and meditational practices, Kundalini Yoga releases anxiety and trauma attached to the energetic body that surrounds the physical body. It is this field, commonly named as an 'aura' that holds wounds. When those wounds are cured, radiance is emanated. Radiance is the magnetic frequency related to attractiveness, love, and light.

Despite achieving a lot of superficial success in life, most people are surrounded by emptiness. Kundalini Yoga helps you believe that living a joyful life is not a luxury, but your birth right. By listening to the whispers of your heart, you will find yourself synchronized with the magnetic force of the universe, which is love. By doing so, your life will be filled with gratitude.

- **You Gain Self-Confidence** - Kundalini Yoga helps you to counter your self-imposed limiting beliefs. It enables you to recognize that you are worthy. By practicing Kundalini yoga, many of life's complications seem less overwhelming. The self-confidence which you gain from Kundalini Yoga rises from deep within. It comes from the feeling of connection to a reservoir of energy, love, and light.

- **Calms Our Mind** - Kundalini Yoga works by suppressing negative thoughts like fear or insecurity, which holds us back.

By hiding the thoughts, our heart and soul gains a chance to flourish. It isn't our mind but our spirit, which shows us the right pathway to our true potential. If we are surrounded by whirling negative thoughts emanating from our mind, the voice of the heart gets drowned out. When our heart is in harmony with our soul's mission, everything flows freely. It opens new doors of intuition and sensitivity. Then, we can get rid of the pain associated with our past and shatter the fears of the future and start to live in the present moment. The sacred mantras and breathwork that is integral to the Kundalini Yoga puts a brake on the racing thoughts, and so calms our mind.

- **Connection with Your Higher Self** - Kundalini Yoga helps you to connect with the universe. By working our body, mind, and soul, we feel connected to higher spiritual truths, which reminds us to trust our potential. This sense of connection keeps us energized and gives us strength and confidence. We start to accept the realities of life and become a more passionate and loving person.

- **Strength and Resilience** - If we do not have enough energy, we feel weak in body and spirit. Our true power comes from our core inner self rather than our muscles, which is what we are made to believe. Practicing Kundalini Yoga regularly assists us in growing a significant core of the prana—or life force, a source of love from inside. By gaining the life force, we gain the ability to cope with the challenges of life effectively.

Exercises like 'Ego Eradicator' help to free the flow of energy through our body and mind.

My dear friend Jasmine became a newly qualified Kundalini Yoga Instructor when I was suffering from post-natal depression. She was a blessing for me as she helped me to recover after what was such a difficult time for me in my relationship. She designed bespoke sessions for me to practice with her, which helped to clear my negative emotions and to reclaim my self-worth.

I would highly recommend that you seek guidance from a qualified Kundalini Yoga Instructor to assist you with your practice as this is such an excellent practice for trauma sufferers.

Anu Verma

By working through and getting rid of the inner energy obstruction, a corresponding release in our life, thoughts, and spirit also ensues. By healing our wounds and vibrating in the frequency of love, we attract more love. This is the law of (Kundalini Yoga) science.

Chapter VII: Emotional Freedom Techniques (EFT)

I became an Emotional Freedom Therapist by training with the EFT Center in London. My primary motivation for this was due to the profound benefits that EFT has bought to me in my life and during my recovery. I am a walking example of the benefits that this magnificent energy healing technique can have.

Even though this method of healing can be self-applied once you know how, I would highly recommend that you seek a qualified EFT Practitioner to assist you in the beginning. This is so they can recommend the best tapping technique that will work for you. They can also offer you a safe environment for you to talk about your circumstances and your concerns.

Emotional Freedom Techniques (EFT) is a curing methodology with significant results for physical and emotional issues. EFT starts with the assumption that emotional stress has a strong relationship with not only psychological but also with human physical problems. Emotional strains negatively impact the natural healing power of the human body. Though EFT can be directly applied against physical ailments, its true potential is visible when personal issues are identified and targeted, too.

EFT is an ongoing process that helps people against old traumas and enables them to cope with upcoming challenges with a positive mindset.

The 'Personal Peace Procedure' provides you with a host of benefits like getting rid of negative beliefs, increasing personal performances, healthy relationships, and vibrant physical health. It is no secret that every single human being on this planet is facing some sort of emotional stress.

EFT Tapping – A Reliable Method

The Chinese Meridian system inspires EFT. While remedies like acupuncture and acupressure focus on solving physical health issues, EFT is used against emotional issues. EFT combines the physical advantages of acupuncture with the cognitive benefits of conventional therapy for faster and more reliable benefits.

EFT – An 'Emotional' Version of Acupuncture

Unlike acupuncture, EFT does not use any needle. Instead, a two-pronged method is used wherein we (1) mentally 'tune in' to the exact problems and (2) stimulate a certain meridian point on the human body by tapping them with our fingers. EFT is considered to be a fast and beneficial therapy for balancing disorders in the meridian system. The basic Tapping process is easy to learn and to use.

The Body's Energy System – Foundation of EFT Tapping

The 5000 years old Chinese discovery of a complex system of energy circuits (meridian system) in the human body is considered the centerpiece of the Eastern health practices. The discovery provides the base for modern-day healing techniques like acupuncture and acupressure.

Emotional Freedom Therapy – An Effective Tool to Heal from Abuse or Trauma

EFT and Trauma

VICTIM 2 VICTOR

Trauma may come in different forms and intensities, and so does your response to it.

Trauma can significantly influence our thinking abilities. It can undermine our thoughts both about ourselves and our very existence. The resulting beliefs can seriously harm our wellbeing and interrupt our everyday life without us recognizing it.

EFT is a useful technique that may be used in various therapies. EFT can not only bring quick relief by overcoming traumatic memories but can also become a helpful tool for working thoroughly on the layers and aspects until the emotional baggage associated with them goes away.

EFT should always be carried out with a trained professional, and once you have learned how to tap on yourself successfully, it can become a useful tool to use by yourself. I have found tapping to be very beneficial, and it has been an ongoing and valuable tool that I have used for my healing. I also learned to tap on myself to curb my sugar addiction and my feelings of sadness from my previous failed relationships.

Trauma sufferers may have physical problems like insomnia, migraines, or even cancer. The lesson to learn is to take traumatic issues seriously and to realize that when an event occurs, which challenges your safety, it can create both emotional as well as physiological responses.

Some people will separate themselves from traumatic events, they will be incapable of accessing any emotion, and often show general symptoms of despair and anxiety.

The following set-up statements can be helpful for trauma sufferers:

- *Even though I have suffered immensely throughout my life, it's ok, because I deeply and completely love and accept myself.*

- *Even though others have hurt me, it's ok because I deeply and completely love and accept myself.*

- *Even though life feels sad and I feel low, it's ok, because I deeply and completely love and accept myself.*

- *Even though I don't feel well, I do not know why it's ok because I deeply and completely love and accept myself.*

- *Even though I have no desire to go back there again, it's ok, because I deeply and completely love and accept myself.*

- *Even though I become nervous when I think about the issue, it's ok, because I deeply and completely love and accept myself.*

- *Even though I am afraid to look at that time again, it's ok, because I completely love and accept myself.*

Post-Traumatic Stress Disorder (PTSD)

People living with PTSD retain the memories associated with past events in their minds as if the circumstances were occurring today. The events may trigger recollections, unnecessary alertness, disturbing dreams, nervousness, and other physiological issues. The sufferers may get lonely and refrain from everyday life routines, as they feel threatened and unsafe. This causes several emotional and physical ailments.

I will now discuss the various EFT methods for working with Trauma:

1. Tearless Trauma

VICTIM 2 VICTOR

2. Movie Technique
3. Telling the Story
4. Imagination Technique

Tearless Trauma

Tearless trauma is a great way to separate the emotions associated with the trauma from the actual traumatic event. The process works as follows:

- Pinpoint a particularly traumatic event from the past, for example, an incident of abuse.

- Convert this to a mini-movie and display it on a wall and think an appropriate title for this movie.

- Think about the level of emotional intensity you would have (on a scale of 0, 1, 2, ... 10) if you watched the movie.

- Make a phrase for the emotion associated with the movie such as "the abuse emotion" and then move to a round of tapping.

- After the round, think again and state a new number for the level of emotional intensity.

- Go for a couple of more rounds of EFT.

- You should start to feel the level of emotional intensity lessen and question yourself, "how would I feel if I were to watch the movie again?"

- If it feels ok, then watch the movie again and stop at any part that still activates an adverse reaction and then tap on this.

- Keep repeating the process until you can watch the complete movie with no emotional connection to it.

The Movie Technique

The Movie technique is similar to the Tearless Trauma Technique. If the trauma does not have very intense effects, then this technique can be used as a start too.

- Create a small movie about a particularly traumatic event.

- Estimate how intense your feelings are when thinking about watching the movie (using a scale of 0 -10).

- If the intensity ratings are high, go back to the Tearless Trauma method.

- If the intensity ratings are low, watch the movie and stop at any point where you feel a high emotional intensity and tap on this.

- Keep repeating the process until the movie is watchable from start to finish, without stimulating an emotional reaction.

Telling the Story

Telling the story is a wonderful method for checking the emotional intensity of your story so far and getting rid of any remaining emotional pain. This technique is generally used when you feel that passion is in an acceptable range.

- Tell your story of the event or memory of the traumatic event.

- As soon as you feel any emotional trouble, stop, and tap on the last statement made.

- Experiment by re-telling that part of the story. You should be able to go past the earlier emotional pain point easily. If not, then there is more to be worked upon.

- Test yourself by telling the complete story from start to end. As soon as you can stay relaxed while telling your story, that is when you know that that the tapping has worked.

Imagination Technique

Many trauma sufferers may not recall the event when the trauma occurred, and they may only have the feelings associated with the trauma. Imagination techniques can be used in these circumstances and to tap on a feeling rather than a visual that is seen during the Tearless Trauma and Movie technique. Check and evaluate how much is stored cognitively. If there is no actual memory, then 'make it up.' The fictitious memory does not have to be an accurate reflection of the thought or the event. What is most important is how you, the trauma sufferer, feels today.

EFT is a great new tool to deal with trauma. It enables you to gain quick relief from unwanted and traumatic encounters. Trauma can be presented at various levels, and there is no fixed method for specific types of trauma. As a rule, the greater the emotional intensity is, then more dissociation is required by using the Movie technique or Tearless Trauma. For those sufferers who may not recall the event, the Imagination technique can be helpful.

Anu Verma

Chapter VIII: How Healing Shifted the Weight

I used food emotionally in my late teens to fill the void in my life, which resulted in me being overweight for several years. When I went to University, I had a much busier lifestyle. I was going out, drinking a lot, and working so I didn't eat as much, and I lost all of my excess weight. In my final year at University, things became stressful because of studying and trying to pass my degree. I stopped being quite so active, and I used food again emotionally. After that, I discovered caffeine pills, which I took to help me work out harder at the gym. I lost a lot of weight again. Only to pile it back on later when I stopped taking the caffeine pills. My weight issue had turned into a rollercoaster and was as up and down like a Yo-Yo. It would stay like that until I had healed.

I had to be able to control my emotions and to get rid of the hurt and sadness that was inside of me before I could become healthier and to not rely on food as an emotional source.

Healing and the Weight Loss

Permanently losing excessive weight and ending the habit of 'emotional eating' is possible after identifying the root cause of the problem, which was inner pain, in my case. After acknowledging and getting rid of this pain, emotional freedom and a healthy body could be attained. Many people underestimate the impact of events which happened in their early life. Unless we address the issues caused by them, negative beliefs and emotions will stay inside of us, continuing to hinder our progress in life and to stop us from reaching the ideal weight for us.

Making the Connection

Dr. Vincent Felitti, who was Director of the obesity clinic at Kaiser Permanente's Department of Preventive Medicine in California, clarified the connection between childhood suffering and obesity in 1985. He was amazed by the fifty percent dropout ratio amongst his patients, after their initial success in losing weight. He investigated why this was happening and discovered that most of those who had dropped out had experienced traumatic childhoods. Most commonly, those were victims of sexual abuse or neglect.

Dr. Felitti noted that the patients considered overeating, and the resulting obesity, as a solution to these more profound problems. They believed that having extra weight made them feel safer. Emotional eating also soothed their feelings of anger, anxiety, and fear. He concluded that to gain a balanced weight and stop overeating, his patients would need to overcome their underlying pain and fear. Dr. Felitti used a questionnaire to help him to understand his patients better. The Center for Disease Control and Prevention used this questionnaire later to confirm the relationship between childhood trauma and physical and mental health issues.

Psychotherapy is also an excellent treatment strategy that can help us to deal with the pain and suffering from our past. This can have a profound impact on our weight, by unblocking the pain and increasing awareness, which will enhance our overall well-being. By addressing the emotional effects of the trauma which we experienced, we can build stronger inner foundations that will help us to use weight reduction strategies more effectively and to lose weight gradually.

Successful Energy Techniques to Lose Weight

Excessive weight is caused by unconsumed energy. In normal circumstances, it can be reduced by exercising and healthy eating habits. If there is a block to the inflow of energy into the body, working out and diet might not obtain the desired results. In cases like this, it's necessary to try the following energy techniques to allow energy to flow freely in the body, and which can, in turn, lead to a reduction in excessive weight.

Let the Energy Flow

We can let our energy flow freely by opening our chakras and energy channels. A host of activities like exercise, yoga, meditation, music, acupuncture, reiki, pranic healing, smudging, and aromatherapy are there to help us to do this.

Bless Your Food

Blessing our food and drink before a meal can be helpful. Setting our intention that in doing this, we will raise the quality of our food. It is a fact that blessing food increases its vibration and alters its molecular structure.

Positive Affirmations

Affirmations are a technique that I practice daily for all aspects of my life, and I will discuss later on in this book. I have set reminders of positive affirmations that come up on my phone numerous times a day and effectively change our state of mind. Try reiterating an assertion as often as we can, as a means of countering any negative views about our body image. One example of a constructive affirmation about bodyweight might be, "I am happy, healthy and joyful at my ideal weight," and you may also try adding a desired weight level to the affirmation if this is preferred.

Appreciate Your Body

It's essential to appreciate the current state of your body. We can't release the excessive energy by simply despising it. We need to love our bodies and believe that we are strong and capable. Sparing a few minutes every morning to look into the mirror and say at least three things about our bodies that we sincerely appreciate adheres to your subconscious. It goes with the saying, "If you say something often enough, you'll believe it. Once we are no longer hostile to the energy surrounding our weight, it can begin to move and eventually be released.

Meditate, Contemplate and Release

We can meditate, contemplate, and release our emotional baggage to the Universe. Using prayer and a declaration to symbolize this, as well as removing the links to those emotions which told us that we were safe because of our weight, is significant. It's time to thank the weight for protecting us and to say goodbye to this extra weight by telling it that it is no longer required.

Practice and See the Results

Using as many of these techniques as possible, we can remove the energy blocks in our bodies and see how effectively the excessive weight goes away. It's also possible to notice many other positive changes in our lives due to following the techniques mentioned above.

Part IV: Making Decisions

Anu Verma

Chapter I: Steps in the Decision-Making Process

Decision-making processes involve more than merely listing our goals. It takes a dedicated amount of time to make a proper decision, so that life will not be negatively impacted. Mastering the decision-making process is a large part of who we are, so I wanted to expand on this topic.

If it wasn't for my decision to want to end the vicious cycle of darkness which I was in, and if it wasn't for my decision to put a stop to the victim mentality which I portrayed for the majority of my life, then my life would never have taken the positive spin which I was in so much need for. I would not be writing this book today and be able to share my story with you if I remained in that victim "Poor Me" mentality. I decided that I was worth more than what life was throwing at me. I decided that I deserved to experience more joy, peace, and happiness in my life.

So, what changed? Well, I can only put this down to waking up one morning and deciding "NO MORE!" Thich was the point in my life when I decided to invest in myself and to work on my spiritual and mental growth.

VICTIM 2 VICTOR

If you think about it, life is a series of decisions. Each step in our life journey should be taken after careful consideration. Moving forward without any or a great deal of thought makes it easy for these decisions to lead to reckless behavior and other choices that cause harm to ourselves or those around us. This was me for the majority of my life.

I made decisions based on emotion or impulsively on the spur of the moment. This led to destructive actions. My suicide attempts came about because of my bad relationships, escape strategies as well as suffering harm. Making proper decisions is a part of healing from trauma, getting our lives back, and doing the right thing. It's best to make choices by identifying a decision and then to gather information to be able to assess alternative resolutions. Using a step-by-step decision-making process can help us to make more deliberate and thoughtful decisions. By writing down the consequences of our choices allows us to organize our thinking, define our alternatives, and enable us to make the best decision possible.

Decision-making processes include; Neuro Associative Conditioning, the Dickens Process, and questioning and pondering before making a significant decision. It is possible to follow an organic, nonlinear path. This is the creative thing to do, but those trying to get their lives back on track rarely have such choices, due to life demands constraints and accountability. A more rigid structure of decision making can lead to a successful and functional end.

The decision-making process could be one of the essential tasks you learn because we are the result of every decision that we make, so understanding the process of effective decision-making could prove wonders in your life. Next time you have a decision to make, try these steps:

- **Define the Decision to be made.** You can't decide until you've determined that there's a decision to make. Do I need to go? Do I want to stay? When it comes to abusive behaviors, should I contact the police, or go with my gut instinct?

- **Bring together all the information that you have before making your decision, gather as many relevant facts as possible.** This implies to both internal and external work. Internal data comes from an evaluation of oneself. In contrast, external data emanates from books, websites, and many others. Evaluate your prior actions. Were they helpful? Were they offensive? Have they helped you to evolve?

- **Classify various courses of action.** Build new approaches using your creativity as well as other relevant data. Consider this step as an information-gathering task. Identify all potentially possible decisions. Be innovative and jot down your options. Your ultimate decision may emerge from an array of options.

- **Evaluate the facts. By using your imagination, generate a checklist of your information.** What will it be like to have each of the options carried out? It may be a complicated method, but evaluate your decisions depending on your set of beliefs. Your one choice that bears some resemblance to reaching your objectives will become evident.

- **Take some action. You have the details.** Now it's time to form the decision and to incorporate it.

- **Don't just blindly enforce your decision.** Observe what's going on and be self-assured that you made the correct decision for yourself.

- **Re-evaluate your decision and its implications.** Has your selection solved the issue? If your choice did not satisfy your expectations or what you needed to accomplish, you would need to go back and repeat the steps.

The important thing is to make decisions based on logic, a plan, and with rational thinking. Don't panic if the end decision turns out to be the wrong one. Use what you have learned from the decision-making process and explore why it didn't work. Think about how you could approach this differently. The process isn't perfect, but only as good as what you put into it.

VICTIM 2 VICTOR

Chapter II: The Dickens Process and Decision Making

Tony Robbins provides an excellent technique for making good decisions. He explains the Dickens Process in his seminars and books. It is a compelling way for anyone to find themselves, and it helped me reach where I am today. The Dickens Process uses simple technology from neuro-linguistic programming (NLP) and other sciences to approach communication, personal development, and psychotherapy. The premise is that there is a significant connection between neurological processes, language or linguistics, and behavioral patterns. They are learned through experience or programming. These behaviors can be changed to help us to achieve happiness and success.

The entire process operates on a subconscious and emotional level. It takes the idea from *A Christmas Carol* by Charles Dickens. When three ghosts appear to Scrooge on Christmas morning, he is shown the past, present, and possible future of what his life will be like if he continues with his miserly and heartless ways. The smells and sights of the past bring a tear to Scrooge's eye. He sees the shadow of his lonely childhood, an uncaring father, and a loving sister. While he also follows the decisions which he made that turned his fiancée against him. She realized that he loved money more than her! Scrooge watches his friends and family become disillusioned with him, and he begins to see how this contributed towards his miserly attitude towards life.

His present ghost is shown in all its graphic glory. Bob Cratchit, Scrooge's clerk, is walking through the snow. He is with his young son, Timmy. The Spirit of the Present takes Scrooge to the Cratchit home, where he can see that the family doesn't have a Christmas Dinner to look forward to. Yet, they are all so positive. Scrooge is unable to cope with their happiness. He hears them talking about him, and there isn't any malice in these conversations. He also sees the excitement growing at his nephew Fred's house. How merry and happy Fred and other members of his family are. Scrooge hasn't been invited to join in with their Christmas festivities.

The Spirit of the Future shows Scrooge at a later date. He is ill and dying alone. Also, a disabled child who is about to be buried, whom we recognize as Timmy: three wealthy gentlemen are laughing about Scrooge's death and at how cheap the funeral will be. He sees his possessions being stolen by his charwoman, to be sold to a fence called Old Joe, who would later sell them for profit. He is shown his shrouded corpse and begs the Spirit not to reveal his face. He finally realizes that he is unwanted and uninvited because of his miserly ways.

Scrooge experiences so much pain from these thoughts and images that he decides to change his life for the better, and for the effects to last forever. The changes he makes affect everything around him in a positive way. He gives away money, forgives debts, and delivers a Christmas dinner to the Cratchit home. No longer is Scrooge lonely or alone. He is soon invited to spend time with others. He has changed into a much kinder person, and so finds a happier life.

In the Dickens Process, we are forced to examine our limiting beliefs and to change them. The process uses the conscious mind to help visualize the possible paths that we can take and attaches real feelings to them. If you think about standing at a crossroads, one side will take you in one direction, or the way you are currently traveling, while the other leads to a possible future. Choosing the right path shows you how your life can change positively for the better and affect everyone around you.

But What Is the Right Path?

Think about your current behavior, and I am just using the following examples. We need to use the worst possible images we can think of for this exercise to work well, such as drinking alcohol to excess or impulsive behavior and possibly damaging ourselves, as I did with thoughts of suicide. See yourself walking along your current road. Imagine how bad it will be in twelve months or five years if you don't change what you do. Think about how poor your health will be and how restrictive your life will turn out. Imagine not being able to play with your children or enjoy your family because of being ill with liver damage. Think about how awful it will feel to lose your home and family if you keep drinking alcohol. Think about how empty life will be if you don't begin to love and trust and cease this abusive behavior. Where will you be if you continue forming relationships with abusive partners who take away all of your power and inner strength?

The point of this exercise is to think of the worst possible outcome your journey could take. Imagine breaking the news to your family that you have a life-threatening illness. See yourself in a position where you are arrested for drink driving and locked up for rehabilitation. Imagine a future where there isn't any love, good relationships, or a stable family. The outcome is that you will never hold your children or watch them grow up. Be realistic and think of yourself experiencing the most profound pain possible if you don't stop this damaging behavior. See your challenging future if you don't change for the better. Feel this future and the surrounding pain. Feel the pain associated with these happenings if you don't change how you are living your life.

Go back to the crossroads and take the 'path to success' instead of the 'path of least resistance.' Think about and write down how you will feel in five years, when you are healthier. You are more successful. You have energy and feel as if you can do anything.

Think about how you will feel in ten years, when you watch your children graduate from college, hold your first grandchild, or go on holiday with your soulmate. Imagine yourself as a happy and healthy person contributing to society—making it a better world. Happiness brings a smile to your face.

Travel back to the crossroads. Think about the consequence of both paths. Feel the acute pain of your current beliefs. Now you can start to throw these actions away and formulate two or three replacement beliefs to use as you move forward. Instead of saying to yourself, "I don't deserve to be in a loving relationship," or "I will carry on drinking. Nothing will happen." Replace this old belief with a new one such as "I am a non-drinker. This is why I am healthier and happier. I am loveable and important. My life is good."

Think repeatedly, how much better you will be if you release your destructive thoughts and actions. Feel the pain of the past and the hopelessness of the present. Look to the future that has a positive vibration, and you will be following the example of Jeff Bezos, who is one of the richest and most successful men in the world. When he makes a decision, he projects his life forward. He says that he takes the path which will minimize his regrets.

If you choose to stay on your current path, think of these questions:

- What will be the cost of my bad habits if I don't change them?
- How will I hurt the people I love, in the future, if I stay on my current path?
- How will this habit affect my future?

Now, ask yourself the following questions. This time when you take the path to make life changes:

- What empowers me to do the right thing for me?
- How will things in my life evolve?
- How will my personal life change?

VICTIM 2 VICTOR

- How can I be happy?

The Dickens Process will transform your life if used as a life-changing tool. It is powerful because it allows us to experience our future selves. To feel the pain involved in keeping to the current path, and to also make decisions based on new information that will guide us to change for the better.

Using the Dickens process shows our conscious mind the paths that we can take, and the consequences of taking them. This tool can be life-changing when we truly apply it. It has transformed the lives of thousands of people, including me.

Make the right decisions by projecting yourself into the role of Scrooge. Are you happy with your current choices? Or is there another path which you could take? You are the only person who can answer these questions. If you empower yourself, you will be successful. This process can be as long as you want it to be or as short. The whole purpose is to make wise decisions and to realize the consequences of those decisions.

Anu Verma

Chapter III: Neuro Associative Conditioning in Decision Making

Neuro Associative Conditioning (NAC) used in decision making can be illustrated as a magnet. One side is negative or pushing us away while the other side is positive, pulling us towards something good. This tool enables us to learn why we are moving away from our current state, and the thoughts that may be pulling us in the direction of our goals. According to Tony Robbins, NAC can create a change in behavior due to decisions being based on the following factors:

- The Need to Avoid Pain.

- The Desire to Gain Pleasure

When we create neuro-associates, both physical and psychological, they are used to determine the immediate meaning of a situation. Is it painful or pleasurable?

When using Neuro-Associative Conditioning (NAC) during decision making:

- **Leverage yourself.** You are at a stage where you realize that you've got to change. You can change, and you will change. You have to get to the stage where it will be unpleasant not to change, so you won't enjoy staying as you are.

- **Disrupt your restricting trend of association.** All behaviors, actions, beliefs, and decisions will either be associated with discomfort or enjoyment. Think of the misery that is caused while choosing to stay in your present situation. Do what it takes to disrupt this activity and create the effect; do something to produce a new outcome.

- **Condition yourself.** Make new trends that encourage you. What is the impact of taking action? What does that do for you? What do you achieve from it? What are the consequences of not taking that action? How would you feel physically and emotionally, realizing that you have been successful?

You have to condition yourself for excellence. Reiterate your steps until they become reliable, acceptable, and a part of daily life. In NAC, you can reach your objectives by asking yourself:

- What do I focus on?

- What do things mean to me?

- What do I need to do to create the desired results?

So, what do we base our decisions on? I will discuss this more in the following section.

Every decision that we make is based upon:

- Our core beliefs, rules, and values.

- Questions that we ask ourselves as we make the decision.

- The emotional state in which we are in. This can either make our decisions or stop our actions.

Beliefs

Beliefs are important because they generalize reality and create a sense of certainty. We rarely question our beliefs since they are based on emotionally charged experiences. A belief is a process of nominalization or believing that something we are used to turns into a decision. Tony Robbins states that belief changing methods involve associating pain to our existing beliefs, and pleasure to the new ones.

It is proven that positive and negative reinforcement works for a limited time, but NAC uses a schedule of reinforcement and concepts that are variable. Asking good quality questions is an essential aspect of Tony Robbins' training. Asking different questions can create doubt and change the focus on what we want or don't want. Additional questions can also change what resources we use. Altering the words in questions can have a significant impact on our quality of life. For example, asking 'why does this always happen to me?' can become 'what can I do to change this?'. Use words and thoughts that are empowering. This has a significant impact on what happens to us, both physically and emotionally. Emotionally charged words can change our experience. Here are some further examples:

- "I am so angry about this situation" can be turned into "I am a bit peeved about this situation." You will notice a difference in how you feel when you do this. Tony Robbins also explains that we can adopt the emotional patterns of others when we use their words.

- The use of metaphors can help us to create a link between the known and the unknown. Metaphors can also limit beliefs, rules, and preconceptions. The analogies which we use cause us to see life in different ways.

    You could ask yourself:

- Why am I committed to reaching this goal?

VICTIM 2 VICTOR

- What attitudes, skills, traits, abilities, and beliefs do I need to develop a successful future?

Decision making can feel overwhelming for some people, but we make decisions hundreds of times a day without even realizing it. These decisions are almost automatic. However, now and then, we will be confronted with a decision that requires more thought and consideration. Why not use the suggested techniques for making these difficult decisions? They will help you to make the right one and have the victorious life that you want.

Other Techniques to Improve the Quality of Life

Other techniques and bio-hacks that I use daily that can increase well-being and improve the quality of life include; goal setting, visualization, incantations and affirmations, rebounding, cold showers, meditation, exercise, journaling, and praying.

Some of these have already been mentioned previously in this book. I will go on now to discuss the other techniques.

How (And Why) Goal Setting Works?

Defining your goal is crucial for success and helps you to pursue goal-seeking actions, so you do not take part in less productive activities. The setting of goals works by boosting your energy and motivation for you to persevere in your actions and to succeed. I always find that writing my goals down is much more effective, and this method has been scientifically proven.

A Harvard Business Study investigated some MBA (Masters in Business Administration) graduates. They found that ten years after these students graduated, the 3% who wrote down their goals ended up earning ten times as much as the other 97% who hadn't written down their goals.

Here are some steps to follow when making goals:

- **Make your goals SMART** - specific, measurable, achievable, realistic, and time.

- **Make your goals visible** - create a vision board and get creative about this.

- **Feel your goals** - write down how you would feel if you were to achieve your goals.

- **Understand your goals** - why do you want to achieve this goal? Understand your 'why'; otherwise, you may not have the motivation to want to follow through with your plan.

- **Take some action** - even if it's just a little step, as this creates a momentum that eventually leads to achieving your bigger goal.

- **Share your goals** - as this keeps you accountable. By sharing your plan, this creates an unknowing commitment to make it happen, and so now it is on you to ensure that it happens.

- **Celebrate** - don't forget to enjoy achieving your goals and to reward yourself for every single step that you take. This is something which many of us fail to do as we take the achievement of goals so seriously and forget to enjoy ourselves during the process.

Visualization

Visualization is the practice of changing your thoughts and using imagination to experience new behaviors and new events, to change the outside world. Patterns can be manifested by creating a vision about what you want. All senses are then used to recreate these new patterns, which eventually become positive habits.

By using the power of creative visualization opens up new opportunities that create positive outcomes, which helps you to make the life that you want.

Visualization Techniques

There are four fundamental advantages of using visualization techniques to reach your goals in life.

- It stimulates your productive subconscious, which generates innovative ideas to accomplish your goals.

- It programs your mind to identify and use the resources you need to achieve your goals.

- It enforces the law of attraction, thereby enabling you to connect with people and resources required to reach your goals.

- It enhances your motivation to enable you to take the required actions for your goals.

Visualization is a simple technique. All you have to do is to sit back, relax, and close your eyes and imagine what you would be looking at if your goals were already accomplished. It is about imagining the ideal situation.

Imagine watching a movie of yourself that shows you doing precisely what you want to improve. Visualize all the possible details associated with the task, such as your body movements and your facial expressions for when you reach your goals. Recreate the whole experience again, looking out through your eyes. Imagining allows you to change your perception, beliefs, and thoughts by activating the 18 billion brain cells and enabling them to work in harmony to achieve your objectives.

Your subconscious will become involved in a process that changes you forever. All you need to do is to invest your time in visualizing, repeating affirmations, and surrounding yourself with people who have constructive personalities. You should read good books and listen to uplifting audio programs that fill your mind with positive energy.

Anu Verma

Harnessing the Subconscious Mind with Visualization Techniques

Visualization is the technique of seeing the objectives as if they were already achieved. It is a fundamental technique used by many successful individuals across the globe. It is significant because it harnesses the power of our subconscious mind.

When we visualize our goals as already completed, this creates a conflict in our subconscious mind, between what we envision and what the reality is. This visualization then triggers the creative forces of our subconscious mind to find the motivation and the solutions to reach your goals.

Visualization also works by programming the Reticular Activating System (RAS), which acts as a mental filter for the eight billion bits of data flowing into our brains at any one time.

The RAS thinks in pictures and not words. Routinely practicing the visualization techniques inserts the images required to start filtering the data into the RAS. As an outcome, your RAS will become attentive to anything that might be helpful for you to achieve your objectives.

Live in the Moment

Daily rituals may be beneficial for you to create the right balance between planning the future and living in the moment. If you practice meditation, then do your visualizations immediately after the meditation. The intensified state attained during the meditation increases the effects of visualization.

For the ultimate impact, read your goals and affirmations out loud. After each one, close your eyes and imagine as if the goals are already accomplished. Most importantly, do not forget to add the feelings and bodily sensations you would experience if you had already attained your objectives. A practical way to quickly return to the present moment would be to focus on your physical senses. By doing so, you will live in the moment as it is impossible to focus on our bodily sensations and be in the future or the past, both at the same time.

Cold Showers

I learned about the benefits of cold showers during my personal development seminars, also inspired by David Goggins. I was taught about stepping out of my comfort zone daily, which would help me to progress and to take more risks to achieve what I wanted to from life. As well as having mental benefits, taking cold showers also has many health benefits such as:

- **Elimination of Extra Fat** - Cold showers help to activate brown fat, which generates heat across the body. Brown fat burns calories so that our body temperature rises. Studies suggest that the temperatures of the cold body can boost brown fat by fifteen times.

- **Immunity is Enhanced** - Research in England states that daily cold showers activate the metabolic rate and white blood cell production, which ultimately improves the strength of our body in its fight against diseases.

- **Improved Circulation of Blood** - Blood circulation is enhanced due to the body pushing the blood to the organs to keep them warm.

- **Enhances the Lymphatic System** - Our lymphatic system ensures that waste is removed from our cells, protecting us from infections.

- **Lowers Anxiety and Stress** - Studies show that cold showers create a healthier nervous system, which helps you to become resilient to anxiety. The amount of uric acid in the blood can be normalized, and glutathione boosted, which lowers stress.

- **Risk of Depression is Decreased** - Cold showers help to decrease depression due to the stimulation of the noradrenaline-emitting "blue spot" on the brain, which is a chemical that is linked to depression.

- **Make Muscle Recovery Fast** - After rigorous fitness training, taking a cold shower increases the circulation of blood. It makes it easier to partly eliminate lactic acid, which accelerates the healing of the body.

- **Benefits for Hair and Skin** - Coldwater usage can help retain certain natural oils in the hair and skin, making hair smoother and shinier.

Incantations

Using incantations and affirmations can have a magical impact on our life. The idea behind using the incantations is that repeatedly saying an empowering phrase to ourselves forces our minds to believe it. Negative words, on the other hand, can hurt our attitude towards life. Incantations are more effective than affirmations because they engage our physiology and sentiments with their powerful phrases. The addition of physical movement transfers these complimentary messages into every cell of our body and forces our brain to trust them.

I always try to substitute negative beliefs or phrases with something more constructive and empowering. For example, here are some positive substitutes for restrictive beliefs:

> *"I am happy! I am in control of how I feel! I choose to be happy right now."*

Whenever we feel bad or unintentionally say something negative or disempowering, it's an opportunity to form a new incantation or affirmation.

A-List of Affirmations and Incantations That I Regularly Use:

- I love myself for who I am.

- I am a joyful person, having lots of positive energy.

- I am grateful for every moment of my life.

- I am at peace.
- I attract only healthy, empowering relationships.

- I give and receive love, effortlessly, and easily.

- I have a fulfilling life.

- My relationship is filled with love and passion.

- I am a source of love and inspiration for my family and friends.

- I am blessed with a beautiful family.

Rebounding Exercise

Rebounding is a type of aerobic exercise that involves jumping on a mini-trampoline, and I like rebounding in the mornings while saying my incantations. This exercise increases both blood and lymph circulation. The lymphatic system is responsible for eliminating harmful toxins from the body. All forms of exercise work on the principle of opposing gravity. Albert Carter, a professional trampolinist and the World's foremost authority on rebound exercise, explained that gravity starts pulling us before we are born and continues to do so until we die. Every part of our body, regardless of where it is, has to cope with or adjust to the gravitational pull of the earth.

Rebound exercises utilize the forces of gravity, as well as the points of acceleration and deceleration. When the springs take over and push the body up into the air, the body adjusts to a weightless condition. This is experienced by the entire body, regardless of where the cells are. When the body is decelerated at the bottom of the bounce, this results in more than one hundred trillion cells having to adjust to an environment that they are not used to.

Anu Verma

Rebounding and the Immune System

The human body has a vast network of lymph channels, and lymph fluid circulates through every part of it. According to Carter, one of the most remarkable benefits of rebound exercise stimulates lymphatic circulation. Thereby boosting the immune system and making it more efficient. The way the lymphatic system works is via the lymphocytes, or white blood cells, which are moved by one-way valves throughout the entire body, the valves all point upwards. By bouncing on a rebounder, jumping on the floor, or using a jump rope, the lymph system is activated. The one-way valves open and close around one hundred times per minute, to circulate the lymph fluid. This gets the white blood cells to areas of the body where they need to be, to remove toxins and waste.

Final Thoughts

Today, I am healing. My life is stable and focused. I am more optimistic. I have a clearer vision of where I am and what I want to achieve. I know who I want to have in my circle of friends and family. Those people who will be spending time with Noah and me. I am mentally strong, blessed, resilient, and lucky to have been through all that I have. It has helped to make me who I am today, which is a strong and independent woman, a mother, and a businesswoman.

I am blessed to have my son growing up to be an intelligent, wise, and funny little boy. My focus now is so much less about me and more about us. I am grateful to have had the mentors in my life who have led me along the right path and enlightened me to become the spiritual being that I am today. I am blessed to understand my spiritual side and the beliefs that have sustained me throughout my journey. I appreciate my real value and the standards that I hold. I am determined not to let anyone into my life who does not meet them. I wish the same for you, and the many blessings I have had.

Victim 2 Victor

I hope that the sharing of my journey and the healing strategies discussed in this book have been helpful tools and those you may wish to use during your healing journey.

During the writing of this book, I am most grateful to my parents, who have helped me in taking care of my son Noah. Without their help, I would not have had the resources available, which has given me space and the valuable time to write.

My Life

This book began with events from my childhood when I was victim of sexual abuse by a family friend at three years of age, and again, at the age of seven, by a relative. I was molested by a college student who threw me into an alley. I was sixteen at the time. This abuse and trauma led to my "wild" and "crazy" behavior. My story continued as I tried to find myself in adolescence as a young adult, and through my University days.

I would like you to understand the further harm that I did to myself because of my "crazy" ways, trying to find myself through drugs, drinking, and sexual behavior. Having read about my life, please think about your own. What are you going through? Were you wild and "crazy," too? Or did you sit and hope that the pain and emotions would go away?

I went from relationship to relationship. A few of them seemed fulfilling, but only for a short time. It usually wasn't long before I could read between the lines and discover what my partners were really like. Looking back now, was I simply trying to validate myself? To my social media and circle of friends, I showed them that I also had someone in my life. I looked toward these relationships to give me the feeling of security that was lacking in my life.

Nevertheless, they didn't keep me safe. Instead, they zapped away my energy and personal power. Another thought that came to me when I had finished writing this book was that I was meant to go through my destructive journey to write this book in hopes of helping others who have gone through or who are going through a similar journey. What had I learned from my journey? I know that I will not jump lightly into a relationship again. I have Noah to consider, and I want to honor myself as a woman.

My travels have been one of the highlights of my life. My first around the world trip took me sixteen months when I traveled through Australia and Southeast Asia. What I saw gave me an appreciation for our beautiful world. That is populated with remarkable people.

Another highlight was, of course, having Noah. He is a beautiful addition to my life, and his presence in my life keeps me grounded. Before I make any decision, I need to consider my son and his part in my life. This helps me to follow the techniques that I have learned on my healing journey. I use the Dickens' model of decision making. I think about the consequences of what I am doing or am maybe about to do. I am confident then that my decisions are right.

Sexual Abuse and Trauma

If you have been sexually abused, please do not suffer alone. Statistics say that one out of every four girls, and one out of six boys, will be or have been sexually abused by the time they reach eighteen. Most of these abusive situations will happen because of a family member or someone that the child knows; sad statistics, and not one that I am proud to be a part of.

All sexual abuse is traumatic and damaging. The trauma doesn't stop when the abuse does. Most victims who have suffered abuse as a child still feel the effects of it when they are an adult. It is, however, possible to heal and, in my case, to thrive. To become successful and happy. A feeling of satisfaction comes with this. Being complete. Having love and trust in relationships and the simplest of pleasure... Just being you.

VICTIM 2 VICTOR

Time heals all wounds, according to the old saying. Perhaps instead, we should use slightly different words? Time dulls all wounds. Healing from child sexual abuse or any abuse takes determination, dedication, and hard work. If you are committed to healing from your childhood trauma, miracles can and do happen.

Healing from childhood, adolescence, or even adult trauma takes more than just you. You must tell your story to someone else. To get validation for the pain which you are feeling. You cannot heal if you keep your abuse a secret or if you isolate yourself. There are many tools that you can use for healing, including therapy and talking about the abuse. A great way to heal is to journal and to write down what you have experienced. When you write down your trauma, you can figure out how you feel, handle the situation, and what you need to do. All these questions can be answered by just writing them down.

Go one step further and talk it through with someone else. I believe that my therapist, Marie, saved my life. She gave me tools like tapping in Emotional Freedom Therapy and my Reiki energies, to help me get through the pain of my childhood and adolescent experience. We wrote down what I had gone through in my relationships with others. As I talked and wrote about these experiences, I understood myself better and could see what I needed to do to turn my script into an empowering one.

I want to give credit for who I am today to Tony Robbins, his inspiration and teachings. It was his decision-making process and self-awareness programs that helped me develop and grow beyond the person that I used to be. Tony Robbins' programs focus on learning to understand how to control thoughts and realizing that we are in full control of our state and that our mind, body, and emotions are interconnected. We can use mind-body techniques to bring more understanding into our lives. Mind-body techniques also influence our feelings. I have learned to embrace living in the moment and become adept at maintaining my self-awareness in any circumstance. Studies and research have shown that the more we are in control of our lives, the more productive we can feel. If we embrace existence in the present, we are well on the way to controlling our minds.

If you have ever felt that your mind is out of control and anxious thoughts are crowding out the good ones, think deeply. Control your mind through meditation as this is a natural way to calm and to center yourself. The discipline behind meditation is that we only focus on one thought at a time. When we are meditating, we are drawing our focus to something calming, which may be our breath or a mantra that we love. Meditation requires repetition to master, and as we find mindfulness, it feels more natural, meaning that we are well on our way to controlling our minds and thoughts. Tony Robbins also promotes recognizing our limiting beliefs; the beliefs which are holding us back are limited, the beliefs which we believe to be accurate, and the beliefs that have been instilled into our minds from a young age or those which are due to conditioning. We can reset our limiting beliefs so that we start to believe in ourselves and believe that anything is achievable if we set our minds to it. We have infinite potential.

Taking control of the mind and building intention into our thought processes takes us into a state where we want to take positive action, instead of continually thinking about what is wrong and complaining. I have learned through this work, and through my therapy, and my studies, precisely what trauma is. With this knowledge, I have been able to combat the trauma which I experienced as a child and as a young girl, and then the trauma which I later brought upon myself.

I highly recommend learning about the healing powers of Reiki and Emotional Freedom Therapy. Find your spirituality through meditation and by practicing yoga asanas. There are so many useful techniques in this world to help us to heal from our trauma. I am not saying that it will be easy. It isn't. It takes years of work, and continuing work, to heal from trauma. Nevertheless, you can do it.

All it takes is for someone to care for you, like how Marie cared for me. Someone to guide you, as Tony Robbins has with me, and someone to love you, like my son, Noah loves me. Once you find these elements in your life, then you, too, can heal from the trauma of the past. You will find a way out of abusive and destructive relationships.

I am complete and grounded. No matter what I have been through, I am still here. I have a long history of victory. My name is Anu. I am a Victor - Not a victim.

Anu Verma

ABOUT THE AUTHOR

I was born in Coventry, England, but have also lived in Manchester, where I studied at University, and in Bournemouth, where my son was born. I hold a BSc Honors in Physiology and Health and MSc Degree in Sports Science, and I also have a Cambridge Qualification in teaching English as a Foreign Language.

My working life has revolved around teaching, both at home and abroad, where I have taught in Thailand for a time, and I also run an online course for students preparing for the UK Grammar School Entrance Exams. I have also had a long-standing career in Medical, Healthcare, and Scientific sales.

It has been my experiences of childhood abuse that has shaped me as a person, first threatening to destroy me and then revealing a path to freedom and happiness that I thought I would never find.

I explore this path in my book, hoping that it will also help others find themselves how I did, through travel, self-help, and a determination to cast off my damaging past.

When I am not working, writing, or teaching, I am likely making memories with my family, reading amazing books, meditating, practicing yoga, helping others, going for long walks, and keeping fit. My heartfelt love for traveling manifested itself in not one, but two long backpacking trips around the world when I went skydiving in Cairns, immersed myself in a shamanic village in the Philippines and volunteered at a school in Nepal. I yearn to travel the world, long for crazy adventures, and look forward to fulfilling my endearing wishes in the near future.

VICTIM 2 VICTOR

I am ambitious and want to use my skills and life experiences to improve the lives of others. I love to work with children, as they are our future, and I want to work with the vulnerable who are suffering or those who have suffered from abuse. I hope that my book will reach out to survivors of abuse and affect the lives of those who feel helpless.

Anu Verma

Thank You

Thank you for reading *Victim 2 Victor*. If you found this book to be of value during your journey, please visit the site where you purchased it and write a brief review. Your feedback is important to me and will help other readers decide on whether to read the book too.

Amazon Review links:
https://www.amazon.co.uk/review/create-review?&asin=B08H19PCHP

https://www.amazon.com/review/create-review?&asin=B08H19PCHP

Goodreads Review link:
https://www.goodreads.com/book/show/55544724-victim-2-victor

Facebook Review link:
https://www.facebook.com/victim2victor/reviews/?ref=page_internal

My Website Review link:
https://victim2victor.net/product/victim-2-victor-book/#reviews

If you would like to join my FREE 12-week self-development plan, then please sign up here: https://victim2victor.net/free-12-week-self-discovery-plan/

If you have any comments or questions, then please do not hesitate to email me at anu@victim2victor.net.

Please visit my website https://victim2victor.net/ for further details and to read my many articles on various topics and issues in relation to self-development and growth.

VICTIM 2 VICTOR

You may also follow me on my 'Healing journey' social media channels:

https://www.instagram.com/healing.journeyy/

https://www.facebook.com/healingjourneyy/

https://www.youtube.com/channel/UCzhhmjStavLAZdhKgWjQb0Q

https://twitter.com/HealingJourne13

Recommended Reading List

Should you wish to read more inspirational books, here is my recommended reading list to help you along your journey of growth and self-realization:

Bessel van der Kolk (2015) The Body Keeps the Score: Brain, Mind, and Body in the Healing of Trauma

Coelho Paulo (1993) The Alchemist. 25th anniversary Ed. Hyper Collins.

David Goggins (1998) Can't Hurt Me: Master Your Mind and Defy the Odds. Lioncrest Publishing.

Devine Megan (2017) It's okay That you aren't okay. 1st edition. United States Sound true, Inc.

F. Sider Lucille (2019) Light shines In the Darkness. 1st ed. Front edge Publishing

Frankl Viktor (1946) Man's Searching For meaning. 4th ed. United States: Beacon press.

Greenberg Dennis (1995) Mind over Mood. 2nd ed. Guilford Publishers.

Keller Jeff (1999) Attitude Is Everything. Hyper Collins.

Kennedy, Sandra, Roth Sid (2017). The simplicity of Healing 1st ed. Destiny Image Publishers.

L. Hay Louise (1984) You can Heal your Life. 30th anniversary Ed. United States: Hay house.

Miguel Ruiz Don (1997) The four Agreements. 15th anniversary Ed. United States Amber-Allen Publishing.

Perrakis Athena (2019). The book of blessings and rituals. 1st ed. United States: Fair winds press.

VICTIM 2 VICTOR

Robbins Tony (1991) Awaken The giant Within 1st ed. Free press. Frazier Karen (2017) Crystal for Beginners 1st edition Callisto Media.

Bibliography

I now list the resources which were used to assist me in the writing of this book:

A Guide to Spiritual Healing. (n.d.). [online] Available at: http://www.mysticknowledge.org/27-A_Guide_to_Spiritual_Healing-pdf.pdf [Accessed 2 Sep. 2019].

Beck A.T., Rush A.J., Shaw B.F. & Emery, G. (1979) Cognitive Therapy of Depression. New York: Guilford Press

BJS (n.d.). *Bureau of Justice Statistics (BJS) - Rape and Sexual Assault*. [online] www.bjs.gov. Available at: http://www.bjs.gov/index.cfm?ty=tp&tid=317 [Accessed 5 Sep. 2019].

Brohi, K. (2012). A strategy for future trauma research Trauma Sciences. British Journal of Surgery. *British Journal of Surgery*, [online] 99 (Suppl 1). Available at: https://bjssjournals.onlinelibrary.wiley.com/doi/epdf/10.1002/bjs.7791 [Accessed 5 Sep. 2020].

Decker, G.M. and Potter, P. (2003). What Are the Distinctions Between Reiki and Therapeutic Touch? *Clinical Journal of Oncology Nursing*, 7 (1), pp. 89–91.

Denner, S.S. (2009). The Science of Energy Therapies and Contemplative Practice. *Holistic Nursing Practice*, 23 (6), pp. 315–334.

Desy, P. lila (2019). *What's the Difference Between Reiki and Healing Touch?* [online] Learn Religions. Available at: https://www.learnreligions.com/healing-touch-vs-reiki-1732289.

VICTIM 2 VICTOR

Dr. Andrew Rosen (2019). *What is Trauma - The Center for Treatment of Anxiety and Mood Disorders*. [online] The Center for Treatment of Anxiety and Mood Disorders. Available at: https://centerforanxietydisorders.com/what-is-trauma/.

Edwards, S.D. (2013). Intuition as a Healing Modality: Historical and Contemporary Perspectives. *Journal of Psychology in Africa*, 23(4), pp. 669–673.

Engel, M. (2014). *Does energy healing really work? The Daily News puts four methods to the test*. [online] nydailynews.com. Available at: https://www.nydailynews.com/life-style/health/energy-healing-work-article-1.1872210 [Accessed 8 Sep. 2019].

Eric, P. (2013). *Reconnective Healing, A New Level of Healing*. [online] Healthy Directions. Available at: https://healthydirections.ca/reconnective-healing-a-new-level-of-healing/ [Accessed 9 Sep. 2019].

Good Therapy (n.d.). *Therapy for Abuse Survivors, Survivors of Abuse – Getting Help for Abuse*. [online] www.goodtherapy.org. Available at: https://www.goodtherapy.org/learn-about-therapy/issues/abuse/get-help [Accessed 2 Sep. 2019].

Halder, D., Barik, B.B., Dasgupta, R.K. and Roy, S.D. (2018). AROMA THERAPY: AN ART OF HEALING. *Indian Research Journal of Pharmacy and Science*, 5 (3), pp.1540–1558.

Healing Touch Program™ (2009). *What is Healing Touch?* [online] Healingtouchprogram.com. Available at: https://www.healingtouchprogram.com/about/what-is-healing-touch [Accessed 3 Oct. 2019].

Johnsen, A. and Rehn, M. (2013). Trauma research 2012. *Scandinavian Journal of Trauma, Resuscitation and Emergency Medicine*, 21(S1).

Kai (n.d.). *Energy Healing Therapy – Finding Happiness Within*. [online] WellBeingAlignment. Available at: https://www.wellbeingalignment.com/energy-healing-therapy.html [Accessed 2 Oct. 2019].

Klinic (2013). *Trauma-informed The Trauma Toolkit*. [online] pp. 90–95. Available at: https://trauma-informed.ca/wp-content/uploads/2013/10/Trauma-informed_Toolkit.pdf.

Kraybill, O.G. (2019). *What Is Trauma?* [online] Psychology Today. Available at: https://www.psychologytoday.com/us/blog/expressive-trauma-integration/201901/what-is-trauma.

Leeb, R.T., Lewis, T. and Zolotor, A.J. (2011). A Review of Physical and Mental Health Consequences of Child Abuse and Neglect and Implications for Practice. *American Journal of Lifestyle Medicine*, 5(5), pp. 454–468.

Lees, A.B. (2019). *The Treatment of Choice for Trauma | NAMI: National Alliance on Mental Illness*. [online] Nami.org. Available at: https://www.nami.org/Blogs/NAMI-Blog/April-2019/The-Treatment-of-Choice-for-Trauma [Accessed 2 Sep. 2019].

Levin, J. (2011). Energy healers: who they are and what they do. *Explore (New York, N.Y.)*, [online] 7(1), pp. 13–26. Available at: https://pubmed.ncbi.nlm.nih.gov/21194668/ [Accessed 3 Sep. 2019].

Machtinger, E.L., Cuca, Y.P., Khanna, N., Rose, C.D. and Kimberg, L.S. (2015). From Treatment to Healing: The Promise of Trauma-Informed Primary Care. *Women's Health Issues*, [online] 25 (3), pp. 193–197. Available at:

https://www.whijournal.com/article/S1049-3867(15)00033-X/abstract [Accessed 16 Apr. 2019].

Marie, M. (2012). *Intuitive Self-Healing: Achieve Balance and Wellness Through the Body's Energy Centers.* Sounds True.

Nelson, G. and Caplan, R. (2014). The Prevention of Child Physical Abuse and Neglect: An Update. *Journal of Applied Research on Children: Informing Policy for Children at Risk*, [online] 5 (1). Available at: https://digitalcommons.library.tmc.edu/childrenatrisk/vol5/iss1/3/ [Accessed 2 Sep. 2019].

NHS Choices (2019). *Treatment - Post-traumatic stress disorder (PTSD).* [online] Available at: https://www.nhs.uk/conditions/post-traumatic-stress-disorder-ptsd/treatment/.

Olivo, E. (2006). Energy Medicine. *Oprah.com.* [online] Available at: https://www.oprah.com/health/energy-medicine/all [Accessed 2 Oct. 2019].

Omega Institute for Holistic Studies Research (2017). *5 Alternative Therapies for Treating Trauma.* [online] Omega. Available at: http://test2.eomega.org/article/5-alternative-therapies-for-treating-trauma [Accessed 12 Oct. 2020].

Onderko, K. (2018). *What Is Trauma? - Definition, Symptoms, Responses, Types & Therapy.* [online] Integrated Listening. Available at: https://integratedlistening.com/what-is-trauma/.

REACH Team (2017). *6 Different Types of Abuse - REACH.* [online] REACH. Available at: https://reachma.org/6-different-types-abuse/.

Reinecke, M. A., Dattilio, F. M., & Freeman, A. (Eds.). (2003). *Cognitive therapy with children and adolescents: A casebook for clinical practice* (2nd ed.). The Guilford Press.

Sleat, G. and Willett, K. (2011). Evolution of trauma care in the UK: Current developments and future expectations. *Injury*, 42(8), pp. 838–840.

Sovereign Health Group (2016). *5 ways music therapy helps trauma victims - Sovereign Health Group*. [online] Sovereign Health Group. Available at: https://www.sovcal.com/therapy/5-ways-music-therapy-helps-trauma-victims/.

Susanne M. Dillmann (2011). *Common Therapy Approaches to Help You Heal from Trauma*. [online] GoodTherapy.org Therapy Blog. Available at: https://www.goodtherapy.org/blog/common-therapy-approaches-to-help-you-heal-from-trauma.

Swan, N. (1998). *Exploring the Role of Child Abuse in Later Drug Abuse*. [online] Drugabuse.gov. Available at: https://archives.drugabuse.gov/news-events/nida-notes/1998/07/exploring-role-child-abuse-in-later-drug-abuse.

The Center for Treatment of Anxiety and Mood Disorders (2017). PTSD Treatment Programs | Post-Traumatic Stress Disorder Therapy. *The Center for Treatment of Anxiety and Mood Disorders*. [online] Available at: https://centerforanxietydisorders.com/treatment-programs/post-traumatic-stress-disorders/ [Accessed 12 Sep. 2019].

TNN (2019). *Eight alternative healing therapies that actually work - Times of India*. [online] The Times of India. Available at: https://timesofindia.indiatimes.com/life-style/health-fitness/health-news/8-alternative-healing-therapies-that-actually-work/articleshow/57003663.cms [Accessed 19 Sep. 2019].

Trauma-Informed Care (2014). *Understanding the Impact of Trauma.* [online] Nih.gov. Available at: https://www.ncbi.nlm.nih.gov/books/NBK207191/.

Trivedi, R.R. and Rejani, T.G. (2016). Expressive Therapy with Children who were Sexually Abused: An Overview. *World Journal of Research and Review,* [online] 3(4), p.262882. Available at: https://www.neliti.com/publications/262882/expressive-therapy-with-children-who-were-sexually-abused-an-overview.

VANTAGE POINT (2019). *Energy Healing Techniques by Vantage Point Recovery.* [online] vantagepointrecovery.com. Available at: https://vantagepointrecovery.com/types-of-energy-healing/ [Accessed 12 Oct. 2019].

Wheeler, K. (2007). Psychotherapeutic Strategies for Healing Trauma. *Perspectives in Psychiatric Care,* 43(3), pp.132–141.

Whitmer, M. (2014). *Energy Therapy: Types of Energy Healing Techniques.* [online] Mesothelioma Center - Vital Services for Cancer Patients & Families. Available at: https://www.asbestos.com/treatment/alternative/energy-therapies/.

Wikipedia (n.d.). *Child abuse - Wikipedia.* [online] en.m.wikipedia.org. Available at: https://en.m.wikipedia.org/wiki/Child_abuse [Accessed 2 Sep. 2019].

Wilson, J. (2014). *Trauma, Transformation, and Healing. An Integrated Approach to Theory Research & Post Traumatic Therapy.* Routledge.

Wodzianski, J. (2018). *Talking Therapy and Abuse Survivors: Does it Help or Hinder the Healing Process? | isurvive.org.* [online] isurvive.org. Available at: https://isurvive.org/talking-therapy-and-abuse-survivors-does-it-help-or-hinder-the-healing-process/ [Accessed 3 Sep. 2019].

INDEX

Acupuncture, 131
Acute Stress Disorder, 6, 98
Autonomic Nervous System, 127
Aversion therapy, 122
Behavior Therapy, 122
Beliefs, 192
benefits of Reiki healing, 154
CEREC technology, 67
Childhood Sexual Abuse, 90
Child's Pose. Yoga Poses
childtrauma.org, 91
Cognitive Behavioral Play Therapy, 123
complex post-traumatic stress disorder, 90
Complex Trauma, 106
Conscious Mind, 126
Crystals, 151
Decision-making, 181, 182
developmental trauma, 13, 105
Dickens Process, 7, 182, 185, 186, 189
Downward-Facing Dog. *Yoga Poses*, *Yoga Poses*
Dr. Amy Naugle, 22
Educational neglect, 86
EFT Tapping, 169
Emotional neglect, 86
Energy healing, iii, 149
Ericksonian Hypnotherapy' method, 129
Exposure Therapy, 130
Extended Puppy Pose. *Yoga Poses*, *Yoga Poses*
Eye Movement Desensitization, 6, 117
four types of neglect, 86
Goal Setting, 193
Group Therapy, 131
Hypnosis, 124
hypnotherapist, 69, 128, 129
Hypnotherapy, 123
Hypnotic Suggestions, 128
Imagery, 6, 118, 119
Imagination Technique, 174
Incantations, 199
Intergenerational Trauma, 105
Journaling, 139
Life Skills, 7, 146
Margaret Thatcher, 5, 6
Medical neglect, 86
meditation, 34, 55, 59, 69, 70, 72, 73, 76, 80, 132, 150, 158, 159, 162, 178, 193, 197, 205
Metaphors, 129
Nagarjuna Kadampa Meditation Center, 70
National Violence Against Women Prevention Research Center, 22
Neuro Associative Conditioning, 182
Neuro-Associative Conditioning, 190
Neurofeedback, 130
neuro-linguistic programming, 185
paedophilia, 12
Parts of Human Mind, 126
pedophilia, 12
Physical abuse, 82, 133, 138
Physical neglect, 86
Post Traumatic Stress Disorder, 92
Psychedelic Therapy, 6, 120
Psychological Abuse, 85
Psychotherapy, 177
PTSD, 6, 86, 90, 92, 93, 98, 99, 100, 101, 103, 110, 113, 121, 123, 130, 131, 133, 159, 160, 161, 171, 215, 217
rape, 45, 46, 56, 57, 58, 82, 84, 91, 93, 94, 97, 98, 138

Rape, 88
Rebounding Exercise, 200
Reflexology, 150
Reiki, 7, ii, iii, 67, 69, 76, 78, 150, 152, 153, 154, 155, 156, 204, 205, 212, 213
Reiki Master, ii, iii, 67, 69, 78, 152
Reticular Activating System, 196
sexual assault, 93
sexual violence, 14, 93
sexually abused, 9, 18, 90, 94, 100, 109, 133, 202, 203
signs of physical abuse, 83
Signs of sexual abuse, 84
Smudging, 151
Social Withdrawal, 103
Sodomy, 89
Subconscious Mind, 127
Suicide, 22
symptoms of abuse, 83
System Desensitization, 6, 121
Tearless Trauma, 172

Tera-Mai Seichem Reiki Master, 67
the American Academy of Child & Adolescent Psychiatry, 100
The American Academy of Experts in Traumatic Stress, 92
The Center for Disease Control, 177
The Movie Technique, 173
The Truth Project, 90
Tony Robbins, 4, 6, ii, iii, 69, 78, 79, 185, 190, 192, 204, 205
Trauma, 5, 6, 7, 4, 78, 81, 89, 96, 97, 98, 101, 102, 103, 105, 106, 108, 111, 114, 131, 135, 158, 159, 160, 161, 170, 172, 173, 174, 203, 210, 212, 213, 214, 215, 216, 217, 218
Trauma-focused Cognitive Behaviors Therapy, 135
Visualization Techniques, 7, 195, 196
WhatsApp, 67
World Health Organization, 90
Yoga Poses, 162

Anu Verma